Faith & Practice

**THE BOOK OF DISCIPLINE OF
THE OHIO VALLEY YEARLY MEETING OF
THE RELIGIOUS SOCIETY OF FRIENDS**

2020 Edition

© Ohio Valley Yearly Meeting, 2020

Ohio Valley Yearly Meeting received inspiration and adapted language from materials in the Suggested Reading List and from the following Friends Disciplines:

Britain Yearly Meeting (1999)
Iowa Yearly Meeting of Friends (Conservative) Discipline (1974)
London Yearly Meeting Christian Faith and Practice (1960)
New England Yearly Meeting (1985)
Pacific Yearly Meeting: Faith and Practice (1973)
Philadelphia Yearly Meeting: Faith and Practice (1998)

ISBN 978-1-7363201-0-5 (hardcover)
ISBN 978-1-7363201-1-2 (paperback)
ISBN 978-1-7363201-2-9 (ebook)

www.ovym.org

TABLE OF CONTENTS

Introduction 1
Listening to the Spirit 3
   Meeting for Worship 3
      Preparation for Worship 3
      Waiting Worship 3
      Vocal Ministry 4
   Corporate Discernment 5
   Individual Spiritual Disciplines 6
      Prayer 6
      Scriptures & Other Spiritual Writings 6
   Other Spiritual Practices 7
      Worship Sharing 7
      Clearness Committees 9
      Spiritual Friendships 10

Principles and Application 11
   Divine Relationship 12
   Quaker Testimonies 13
      Community 15
      Equality 16
         Affirmation of Marriage Equality 18
      Integrity 18
      Peace 19
      Seeking Harmony with Creation 22
      Simplicity 23
   Close Relationships 24
      Friendship 25
      Sexuality 25
      Marriages and Other Steadfast Commitments ... 26
         Supporting Families 26
         Sharing a home 27
         Nurturing children 27
         Special needs and long-term illness 29

Table of Contents

Addiction in a home 29
Abuse in a home 29
Divorce 30
Death 30
Preparation for Death 30
Bereavement 31
Stewardship 32
Work in the World 33
Accumulation of Wealth & Payment of Debts 33
Serving as a Trustee 34
Alcohol, Drugs, & Tobacco 34
Recreation and Use of Time 35
Civic Responsibilities 35
Citizenship 35
Obedience to Law & Civil Disobedience 35
Treatment of Civic Offenders 36

Meeting Structure, Function and Procedures 37
General Business Procedure 37
Establishment of Meetings 39
Discontinuance of Meetings 41
Reversion of Property 42
The Monthly Meeting 43
Organization 44
Officers 44
Meeting Trustees 45
Committees 45
Fostering the Meeting for Worship 46
Pastoral Care 47
Religious Education 49
Education of Children, Adolescents, and Young Adults
.... 49
Outreach 49
State of the Meeting Report 50

ii

Table of Contents

Membership 51
    Attenders 52
    Preparation for Membership 52
    Membership Application Process 53
    Youth Membership 54
    Dual Membership 56
    Sojourning Membership 56
    Transfer of Membership 57
    Termination of Membership 57
        Resignation 58
        Loss of Interest 58
        Disownment 59
        Appeals 59
    Marriage Procedure 60
        Clearness Committee for Marriage 62
        Marriage of Two Non-Members 62
        Marriage Ceremony 63
        Form of Certificate 63
    Meeting Records 64
    Recorded Ministers 66
    Ecclesiastical Endorsement 66
    Intervisitation 67
        Letter of Introduction 67
        Traveling Minute 67
    Meeting Funds 68
    Incorporation 68
    Meeting Trusts & Property Titles 69
    Burial Grounds 69

Quarterly Meeting 69

Yearly Meeting 70
    Executive Committee 71
        Duties 71
        Meetings 72
        Minutes 72
        Method of Appointment 72
    Nominating Committee 73
    Annual Statistical Report 73

Table of Contents

Queries 73
Faith & Practice Revision 75
Other Quaker Organizations 76
   Friends General Conference 76
   American Friends Service Committee 77
   Friends World Committee for Consultation 78
   Quaker United Nations Office 79
   Friends Committee on National Legislation 79
   Friends Journal 79
   Quaker Earthcare Witness 80
A Brief History 81
   The Beginnings of Quakerism 81
   Friends in the American Colonies 85
   The Second Period of Quakerism 86
   History of Ohio Valley Yearly Meeting 88
Glossary 91
Suggested Reading List 101
Notes 103
Index 105

INTRODUCTION

Dearly beloved Friends, these things we do not lay upon you as a rule or form to walk by, but that all with the measure of light which is pure and holy may be guided, and so in the light walking and abiding these may be fulfilled in the Spirit,—not in the letter, for the letter killeth, but the Spirit giveth life (The Elders at Balby).[1]

The Ohio Valley Yearly Meeting of the Religious Society of Friends holds as the basis of its faith the belief that divine truth and the gift of God's presence are available to all people in all ages. The indwelling presence of God implies the equal worth of all members of the human family and the capacity in all to discern spiritual truth and to hold direct communion with the Divine Spirit.

Our central shared spiritual experience is the meeting for worship. Friends seek to experience communion with the Divine and—through the Divine—with one another. No mediator, rite, or outward sacrament is a necessary condition of worship. All that is necessary is a seeking spirit on the part of the worshiper. When Friends gather in meeting for worship, we begin in silent expectancy awaiting the guidance and inspiration of the Spirit. This guidance is communicated directly to individuals and may be brought forward in vocal ministry. Through our shared experience of worship, we gain a clearer vision of God and God's will for our lives.

In like manner, our meetings for business are conducted under the discipline of worship, by which we seek neither majority rule nor a secular consensus but rather a clear understanding of the will of God for that group of Friends gathered at a particular time and place.

Because we experience that the Divine lies deeper than words, we have no formal creed. Friends have used various expressions—

Introduction

the Light Within, the Light, or Spirit of Christ, the Holy Spirit, the Word, that of God, Truth, Power, Seed, the Ground of Being, and many more—to describe our experience of the Divine Life. The tapestry of our beliefs is informed by the life and teaching of Jesus of Nazareth, Christian writings, the spiritual insights of many faiths and their inspired teachers, and a sense of awe in contemplating the natural world. What binds us together as a spiritual community is not uniformity of belief, but rather our sense of a common journey on a shared path, seeking the guidance of the Light. Our diversity strengthens us as we walk this path of love, compassion, and justice.

We are called to cultivate a close relationship with the Divine Spirit through daily spiritual practices and frequent occasions of group worship. We seek the continuing revelation of God's will and we test individual leadings and conceptions of Truth with the collective witness of Friends past and present. We endeavor to live in accord with the Quaker testimonies. These practical expressions of our faith flow from the belief that love, the manifestation of the Divine Spirit, is the most potent influence that can be applied in the affairs of life. Friends welcome into fellowship all those who sincerely try to follow the Inward Light.

LISTENING TO THE SPIRIT

The essential purpose of a religious organization is to foster and encourage the spiritual life and to bring the human spirit into intimate relation with the Divine Spirit. Our spiritual life may and should be developed through works of righteousness and loving kindness. Religious communities also provide organized opportunities for the development of our spiritual natures and for the constant renewal of our strength at the Divine Source.

Meeting for Worship

A Quaker meeting for worship is held with minimal preplanning. Friends gather at a specified time and place in silence, waiting on God and the leadings of the Holy Spirit. Some Friends may be given vocal messages to share with the meeting or it may be entirely silent.

PREPARATION FOR WORSHIP

Frequent intentional periods of private reflection, meditation, reading the Bible, Quaker writings or other inspirational texts, prayer, and appreciation of beauty and nature are recommended throughout the week as preparation for the meeting hour. Constant openness to be guided by the Inward Light and a commitment to live with integrity are preparation for worship and ministry. In addition, our ability to hear not just the words uttered, but the spiritual messages underlying those outward expressions is enhanced by our times of preparation.

WAITING WORSHIP

The basis of meeting for worship is silent waiting for direct communion with God and each other. It provides an opportunity to step together into the holy stream, making it a time of expectant

Listening to the Spirit

waiting for the leadings of the Divine Spirit for us as individuals and for the community of worshippers.

Simply gathering in outward silence is not enough. Each individual must consciously and humbly seek for a renewed sense of the inward power of the Spirit. From the depths of that stillness comes an awareness of the presence of God. In this experience individuals will not only find direction for their own lives and strength for their needs but may also feel an urge to share with others the openings that come to them. As worshippers seek to be led into deeper understandings, and pray to become more obedient to the Light Within, their shared communion with the Divine releases the riches of the Spirit.

True ministry, whether vocal or silent, is offering ourselves—body, mind, and soul—to do God's will. During silent waiting, the flow of the Divine Spirit from heart to heart is often felt. Worshippers gather in a spirit of silent prayer with a willingness to give, as well as to receive, so that the full possibilities of the meeting hour can be reached and its influence extended throughout the community from week to week.

VOCAL MINISTRY

To awaken and sustain the spirit of worship, spiritual sensitivity must always be the first requirement for ministry. The Society of Friends believes that vocal ministry should arise out of a call to service. Such a call is a divinely inspired revelation of truth that speaks to a need in the meeting. Our conviction is that the Spirit of God is in all and that vocal utterance comes when this Spirit works within us. As each person listens for God's counsel, the individual receives the inflowing power of divine love. The Friend must then discern whether this message is for themselves or for the meeting as a whole.

We do not set anyone apart to offer ministry in our meetings. The varying needs of a meeting are best supplied by different personalities, and a meeting is enriched by the sharing of any person's living experience of God. Responsibility rests on all to be ready and willing to take part in worship under a due sense of divine prompting.

The call to ministry is a normal experience. It may come to any earnest seeker for divine help and can be recognized by a persistent inner urge to share religious experience or spiritual aspiration. Those who are timid or unaccustomed to speaking should have faith that God will strengthen them to give their messages. Experienced speakers should be watchful not to share at undue length or frequency. It is helpful to allow a period of silent reflection between vocal expressions.

As loving attenders at our meetings for worship, it is up to us to listen for what an awkward minister is attempting to say. We need to attempt to understand the meaning underlying uncomfortable words in order to feel the minister's message. Censoring or dismissing another's message because of their word choice does not build spiritual unity or growth in the community.

Children are a part of the meeting and may be called on occasion to offer ministry to the meeting. Moreover, Friends should be aware of the presence of younger people when choosing what words to use in their ministry.

Corporate Discernment

> *The property of the true church government, and the practice and path of the true church in these our days, is to leave the conscience to its full liberty in the Lord; to preserve it single and entire for the Lord, and to seek unity in the Light and in the Spirit, walking sweetly and harmoniously together in the midst of differing practices (Isaac Penington).*[2]

Listening to the Spirit

Our business meetings are conducted under the immediate guidance of the Holy Spirit. Friends believe that everyone has direct access to the voice of the Inward Teacher and thus anyone may be an instrument through which we can receive God's guidance. As such, we need to listen attentively and with forbearance to all messages that are given in the course of a business meeting. Moreover, we have learned that the discernment of the group is usually superior to that of the individual in seeking to understand where God is leading us as a body. (For a description of the business process, see **General Business** Procedure on page 37.)

Individual Spiritual Disciplines

PRAYER

Prayer is the aspiration of the soul. It is our communion with God and is essential to religious life. Prayer may be experienced throughout the day by noticing that of God in one another and in the natural world. The result of prayer becomes apparent in the more deeply centered lives of those who are constant in its exercise. We should cultivate individually the habit of turning to God at all times and of seeking divine guidance in all things. Vocal prayer, when prompted by a deep concern and a sense of human need, is a vital part of worship and often helps those assembled to come into consciousness of God's presence.

SCRIPTURES & OTHER SPIRITUAL WRITINGS

> *There is a principle which is pure, placed in the human mind, which in different places and ages hath had different names. It is, however, pure and proceeds from God. It is deep and inward, confined to no forms of religion nor excluded from any, where the heart stands in perfect sincerity (John Woolman).*[3]

Listening to the Spirit

We earnestly recommend the reverent, habitual, and intelligent reading of the Bible and other inspirational writings for spiritual enrichment. We would ground our children solidly in the Judeo-Christian faith while yet remembering the words of John Woolman.

God has spoken to all generations. Prophets and teachers to whom the message has come with more convincing power have recorded these revelations of Truth. The hopes and fears, aspirations, and trust of devout people whose quest was to find God and obey God's teaching are recorded in the Bible and other spiritual writings.

The progressive development which it records leads us from the primitive conceptions of an early religion to the culminating gospel of forgiveness, love, and fellowship as taught and lived by Jesus.

Many of the various literary forms of the Bible are characterized by dignity, sublimity, and beauty. Its spirit transcends the medium of expression. Through the ages people have turned to the Bible for consolation, for strength, and for hope. Our prayers are often uttered in its language and our ideals of social justice are found in its pages.

Other Spiritual Practices

WORSHIP SHARING

Worship sharing is an opportunity for a group of Friends to focus on a particular question under divine guidance. This may be an especially troubling issue within a meeting or a query inviting personal reflection. It can be helpful in a variety of situations when we need a chance to share more deeply with each other than we would in ordinary conversation. Worship sharing opens a sacred space, where we can take down our usual defenses and encounter each other in that which is eternal. In that place, we are mindful of

Listening to the Spirit

the personal nature of the sharing and do not repeat outside the session things that are meant only for that particular time.

We come to meeting for worship open to speaking or not speaking, as we are led. In worship sharing we come aware that we will probably speak, although no one is compelled to do so. We enter as though we have all the time in the world—yet mindful of how much time we actually have. All are individually responsible for keeping within the available time, so that each has an opportunity to speak and to listen to what others say. It is often helpful for one participant to be aware of the time and to gently shepherd those present.

We speak only for ourselves and from our own experiences, attempting to distill the promptings of the Spirit into a single statement. Our goal is to speak from the heart; not to answer, discuss, or correct one another, which can serve to separate us from one another and from what is said. Each person should speak only once before all have had an opportunity to do so. This opens space for those who are more reticent to share in the process.

While others are speaking, we are open and attentive. We listen to others as children of God, each one a unique gift to us. We try to hear how the Holy Spirit might be speaking to us personally in the other's words, in their situations, even—and especially—when we find ourselves resistant to those words.

As each person finishes speaking, we allow time in contemplation to take in what has been said and to be sure we have truly heard it. This is an opportunity to identify our resonances and resistances before the next person speaks.

As we listen, we may become mindful of a pattern emerging that reflects the movement of the Spirit among us.

Listening to the Spirit

CLEARNESS COMMITTEES

A clearness committee is created when one or more individuals who are seeking clearness ask three or four other Friends to join with them in a spirit of worship, listening, and loving concern. All members and attenders can request a clearness committee from the meeting that they attend.

Traditionally, clearness committees involved consideration of a concern that might be brought formally under a meeting's care and discernment, such as a request for membership or marriage. In these cases, clearness is sought on behalf of both the meeting and the individual(s). (See **Clearness Committee for Marriage** on page 62 and **Membership Application Process** on page 53.)

Clearness committees may also be used to test personal decisions or transitions. The clearness process may be used to discern the nature of a call to public ministry or witness, whether there is a leading of the Spirit, what faithfulness requires, and whether way is open for responding. This process may reveal that submitting the leading to the meeting's care and accountability would be empowering.

Clearness is a collective process of discerning the leadings of the Inward Light. The process is simple. Members of the committee ask questions that might help the seeker's own discernment—without offering advice, sharing personal anecdotes, or counseling. Testing for clearness is a spiritual exercise. It requires a spirit of openness and trust in the guidance of the Holy Spirit.

A clearness process that has been favored by the movement of the Spirit may produce an unexpected or surprising outcome.

Listening to the Spirit

SPIRITUAL FRIENDSHIPS

A spiritual friendship is an intentional, structured relationship between two or more people committed to helping one another in their spiritual journeys. The focus is on each person's relationship with God and how God's presence may be felt—or not felt—in their lives.

The establishment of spiritual friendships can deepen and strengthen the life of a meeting. Two or perhaps three people agree to meet for at least two hours on a regular basis. The topics of conversation can vary according to the needs of each person, but the overall goal is to support one another during conversations through deep, Spirit-led listening and to pray for one another between gatherings. Often such friendships last for years.

For more on forming spiritual friendships, consult *More Than Equals: Spiritual Friendships* (Pendle Hill Pamphlet 345) where Australian Friend, Trish Roberts explores the particular ways that Friends can benefit from such relationships. She grounds the practice in Quaker theology and suggests three key features: confidentiality, mutuality, and intentionality.

PRINCIPLES AND APPLICATION

The fundamental faith of the Religious Society of Friends leads to a way of life. In the application of the principles of Truth to daily life we acknowledge as supreme the authority of the Divine Spirit in the individual soul. No outward authority can replace it. We must be true to our understanding of God's guidance.

Individuals ought, however, to test their conceptions of Truth by comparison with the individual and collective religious experiences of others (see **Clearness Committees** on page 9). Such experiences are found in rich abundance in the Bible and in the lives of spiritual men and women in all ages, the highest expression being in the life and teachings of Jesus.

Jesus lived a life of love. He taught that love is the motivating power of life, and that its application is the solution of all the problems of life. To the challenge of this way of life the Spirit within us responds. We accept and make the ideals of Jesus our own. We accept the application of the principle of love as the practical way of life and the perfect goal short of which we cannot be satisfied. The bond of our religious fellowship is an experience in the soul that God is love.

Truth is an ever-opening pathway which, if followed, will lead us to higher levels of life and conduct. Its applications vary according to the changing conditions of life. By the faithfulness of each individual in seeking for the Truth and making it known to others when found (see **Meeting for Worship** on page 3), we are able to advance.

It has been our experience that the guidance of the Divine Spirit has in great measure led us as a group to similar standards of life and conduct. In trying to understand the will of God, a statement of these standards is made as a guide for all who wish to compare their individual revelations to those of others.

Principles and Application

We believe that a vital faith must have its application in life. We would place the emphasis not on works alone, nor on faith alone, but upon the union of faith and works.

Divine Relationship

It is our common experience that communion with God is a fundamental need of the human soul. Constant listening for the promptings of the Divine Spirit and seeking to follow it in every relation of life will lead inevitably to spiritual growth.

If we are faithful followers of Jesus, we may expect at times to differ from the practice of others. Having in mind that truth in all ages has been advanced by the courageous example of spiritual leaders, Friends are earnestly advised to be faithful to those leadings of the Divine Spirit which they feel they have interpreted truly after mature meditation and consideration.

Our weekly meetings for worship serve a helpful purpose in calling attention at regular intervals to our need for spiritual communion (see **Meeting for Worship** on page 3). They cannot, however, take the place of daily and hourly looking to God for guidance. Nor can any custom of fasting, abstaining from bodily comforts, or other practice take the place of constantly refraining from everything which tends to unfit mind and body for being the temple of the Divine Spirit. The foundation for all our personal life and social relations should be the sufficient and irreplaceable consciousness of God.

Principles and Application

Quaker Testimonies

> *Be patterns, be examples in all countries, places, islands, nations, wherever you come; that your life and conduct may preach among all sorts of people, and to them. Then you will come to walk cheerfully over the world, answering that of God in every one; whereby in them ye may be a blessing, and make the witness of God in them to bless you (George Fox).*[4]

Quaker spirituality is grounded in a direct relationship with the Divine. Quaker testimonies are visible manifestations of our corporate spiritual relationship, flowing naturally from a shared experience of God's call. They are not rules we follow or things we do in order to get close to God but the fruits of faithfulness. As we follow the guidance of the Inward Light, our lives become simpler and our relationships characterized by integrity, equality, and peace. We are drawn into loving community with each other and with all of creation. We become patterns and examples, because testimonies are outward and public acts—shared expressions of the beliefs of the whole community.

For the first 300 years of the Religious Society of Friends, Quakers expressed their inward spiritual relationship through various outward behaviors. These included ministry under the immediate guidance of the Holy Spirit; distinctive manners of dress and speech; and the rejection of professional clergy, outward rites and rituals; and refraining from what they termed "recreations and pastimes of the world."[5] Such corporate witness could be dangerous. In times of persecution, publicly identifying with the Society of Friends exposed some to scorn and harassment, fines, and imprisonment, even death.

What we now call testimonies have evolved over time. For example, Quaker plain dress, which initially only meant avoiding unnecessary ornamentation, later hardened into the classic gray uniforms for men and women. In the middle of the 19th century,

Principles and Application

most Friends came to see that wearing "the plain clothes" was merely a way to enforce outward conformity rather than an expression of an inward spiritual relationship. Today some Friends wear distinctive plain clothes as a personal witness, but most have returned to our earliest understanding of plain dress by adopting a simple, modest appearance.

Continuing revelation also results in new testimonies. For many years, individual Friends felt a personal concern for humanity's relationship with the natural world. More recently, monthly meetings and Ohio Valley Yearly Meeting came to see that this is more than a personal witness. Sustainability is a corporate spiritual imperative, in other words, a Quaker testimony.

The origin of our contemporary concept of "Quaker Testimonies" can be found in the middle of the 20th century writings of Howard Brinton. He proposed that over time Friends had come to realize the social implications of our religious beliefs, and this had resulted in the development of four corporate testimonies—community, harmony, equality, and simplicity. In the intervening years, this list has been modified and expanded in a number of ways by different groups of Friends. In Ohio Valley Yearly Meeting, the Quaker testimonies are generally understood to be simplicity, peace, integrity, community, equality, and harmony with creation. These are broad categories, not an exhaustive list of the ways in which we witness as a religious society. Each will be addressed in a subsection below.

While living our testimonies can be a source of joy, the Spirit has often directed Friends to challenge the customs and standards of the wider society. Faithfulness may require us to act contrary to comfortable and familiar ways. It can lead us into action we would rather avoid, but if we are true to our calling as Friends, we can do no less.

Principles and Application

COMMUNITY

Dear friends, since God so loved us, we also ought to love one another (1 John 4:11).[6]

Our life is love, and peace, and tenderness; and bearing one with another, and forgiving one another, and not laying accusations one against another; but praying one for another, and helping one another up with a tender hand (Isaac Penington).[7]

In a true community we will not choose our companions, for our choices are so often limited by self-serving motives. Instead, our companions will be given to us by grace. Often they will be persons who will upset our settled view of self and world. In fact, we might define true community as the place where the person you least want to live with always lives (Parker J. Palmer).[8]

A well-functioning meeting acts as one, as a body...It means understanding the meeting community as an organism that is responsive to God as a whole, rather than just as a collection of individuals (Fran Taber).[9]

Each of us lives in multiple overlapping and interconnected communities. Some we are born into, while others we choose to join. Each one provides us with an opportunity to test, refine, and express our beliefs, attitudes, and preferences. Claiming membership in a community is a way to define ourselves to others. As we live into that commitment, community can be more than just a group of people. It can embody our testimonies—a way we witness to the world about what we believe to be most important.

A Quaker Community is many things. It is where we seek and worship the divine. It is a body of Friends who provide temporal support and spiritual nurture for each other. It is where we test our sense of what God has called us to do individually and as a people. By shouldering the responsibilities of membership, we declare our willingness to wrestle together with what it means to be a Quaker

Principles and Application

and to help each other put what we discover into practice. It daily tests us to stay centered in compassion as we encounter the varieties of human experience. A Quaker community declares that each has a unique relationship with God and with each other; it challenges us to faithfully live into those relationships. It is where we risk being transformed.

Community life exposes our own and others' foibles and failures. It reminds us to look to the Inward Light for guidance in our everyday lives. God brought our companions to us; living with them in community, we learn and relearn to love and forgive, to be patient, accepting, and generous. It provides a space for us to safely engage with beliefs that are different from our own.

If we only observe those principles within our Quaker community, it can be an excuse to withdraw into ourselves. The testimony of community requires that we also live out what we believe in the wider world.

When community is our testimony, we love our neighbor as ourselves. Our outward actions reveal spiritually-rooted alternatives to the ways of the wider culture—we model growing spiritually and help others do the same. The Quaker Testimony of Community proclaims a different way to live with others. It challenges each of us to put a relationship with God at the center of our lives and to let that bond shape all our relationships with each other and with the larger world.

EQUALITY

For God does not show favoritism (Romans 2:11).

God the Father made no such difference in the first Creation, nor ever since between the male and the female...so also, His Son, Christ Jesus, confirms the same thing (Margaret Fell).[10]

Principles and Application

To consider mankind otherwise than brethren, to think favors are peculiar to one nation and exclude others, plainly supposes a darkness in the understanding. For as God's love is universal, so where the mind is sufficiently influenced by it, it begets a likeness of itself and the heart is enlarged towards all men (John Woolman).[11]

The roots of racial prejudice lie deep within us, and in seeking a solution to the evil results of racial tensions we need to search our own hearts. Our belief in the significance of every individual in the sight of God and his need for an abundant life can guide us even when we shrink before the vastness of the problem (London Yearly Meeting).[12]

Early Friends based their treatment of others on scripture and continuing revelation. In the Bible, they saw that God created and cares for all humans equally. Continuing revelation led Quakers to see that believing in spiritual equality carries implications for how we live our outward lives.

There is that of God in all people and we believe each person has equal access to the divine. This fundamental belief led Friends to appreciate women's spiritual gifts and to reject practices designed to maintain distinctions among social classes. Friends came to recognize that no one could justly hold another in slavery. We are also coming to realize how such unjust inequities are maintained by an unequal distribution of wealth and resources—an inequality that many Friends benefit from. Living out the testimonies requires reexamination in each era. We believe humble, faithful discernment in community will reveal what love requires of us.

Most Friends in Ohio Valley Yearly Meeting have benefited from unearned, often unacknowledged and unrecognized privileges. It is easy to be lulled into believing racism and unearned privilege have been overcome. This can render Friends oblivious to the ways such attitudes influence behavior. Facing these uncomfortable

Principles and Application

realities and assumptions can reveal hidden, unfair, and harmful biases.

To be faithful, Friends must be willing to confront anything in our lives, in our religious society, and in the surrounding culture that unjustly holds one person up and holds another back. We need to live up to our understanding that all are equally children of God. Our calling as Friends is to seek more Light in ourselves and others and let that guide us in testifying to equality by our lives.

Affirmation of Marriage Equality

In recent decades Friends have also come to reject other forms of inequality. In particular, many straight Friends stood with lesbian, gay, bisexual, transgender, and queer Friends in calling for full equality for people of all gender identities and sexual orientations, and for the elimination of legal barriers to marriage and full equality.

INTEGRITY

Above all, my brothers, do not swear—not by heaven or by earth or by anything else. Let your "Yes" be yes, and your "No," no (James 5:12).

Let your lives and conversations preach, that with a measure of the spirit of God you may reach to that of God in all (George Fox).[13]

Fear is a common obstacle to integrity (Philip Gulley).[14]

When we place truth at the center of our lives, we live with integrity. A life of integrity arises from discerning divine truth as best we can and lovingly acting in accordance with that discernment. Integrity is expressed in being truthful, honest, and transparent; in living so that we will not have to be untruthful in the future. These outward signs grow out of ongoing, inward work. Such faithfulness leads to wholeness, to the integration of body, mind, and spirit.

We are limited beings, who often hear the voice of God only faintly. Impatience may tempt us to follow our personal desires.

Principles and Application

Shame, pride, or insecurity can lead us to seek worldly approval. It takes patience and humility to stand still in the Light and to wait for clarity before we act.

We do not have to travel this path alone. Our meeting communities provide encouragement, strength, and companionship in our everyday lives. They can also help us discern the rightness of a perceived leading and provide support and accountability when clearness has been reached. In similar fashion meetings embody integrity when Friends practice discernment together.

When we follow divine guidance, we find the strength and nourishment to be faithful and to speak and act in accordance with truth in all relationships and in all parts of our lives. Integrity is our way of life.

PEACE

From whence come wars and fightings among you? come they not hence, even of your lusts that war in your members? Ye lust, and have not: ye kill, and desire to have, and cannot obtain: ye fight and war, yet ye have not, because ye ask not (James 4:1-2 King James Version).

I told them I lived in the virtue of that life and power that took away the occasion of all wars...I told them I was come into the covenant of peace which was before wars and strife were (George Fox).[15]

Our principle is...to seek peace, and ensue it, and to follow after righteousness and the knowledge of God, seeking the good and welfare, and doing that which tends to the peace of all. All bloody principles and practices we do utterly deny, with all outward wars, and strife, and fightings with outward weapons, for any end, or under any pretense whatsoever, and this is our testimony to the whole world (Declaration from the harmless & innocent people of God, called, Quakers, 1660).[16]

Principles and Application

May we look upon our treasures, and the furniture of our houses, and the garments in which we array ourselves, and try whether the seeds of war have nourishment in these our possessions, or not (John Woolman).[17]

Through continuing revelation, Friends testimonies against war and for peace have evolved over the centuries. At first, Friends simply refused to participate in war or military service. Over time, Quakers came to understand that mere opposition to war was insufficient and were led to work for peace. Our peace testimony has led us individually and corporately to work for the abolition of practices rooted in violence and coercion and to sow the seeds of peace in our lives and in the world.

We live in a society that glorifies war. Friends seek to follow the teaching and example of Jesus in rejecting the use of coercion and violence. We believe that God calls us to live together in the covenant of peace envisioned by George Fox. Our path is grounded in deep spiritual listening for the guidance of the Inward Teacher, in humility and openness to multiple perspectives.

Living this way requires patience, perseverance, and courage. It often results in legal, social, or financial sacrifices. When faced with military registration and conscription, many Friends claim conscientious objector status or refuse any cooperation with the military. Some refuse to pay war taxes or restrict their incomes to avoid the assessment of such taxes. Some Friends voluntarily place themselves in harm's way in order to witness for peace and against oppression and the use of violence. Friends also encourage governments to refrain from military responses to international conflicts and other acts of violence. Quaker organizations like the American Friends Service Committee and Right Sharing of World Resources contribute to building a more peaceful world (see **Other Quaker Organizations** on page 76).

Principles and Application

If violence and war are to be avoided, whether between individuals, groups, or entire nations, their sources must be recognized. The seeds of conflict are in our hearts. Fear, greed, and intolerance wound the human spirit and obscure the Inward Light given to each person. Quaker peace witness seeks to heal these wounds by answering that of God in each person with courage, compassion, and justice.

We believe that God has called us to lead lives of nonviolence, seeking creative alternatives to resolve conflicts when they arise in our lives. The path of peace is in many ways at odds with the world around us and may lead us to act in ways that challenge the values of the dominant culture. On occasion, it may also require patience as we lovingly hold the tension of an as-yet-unresolved conflict, awaiting a transformation of mind and heart within others and within ourselves.

Friends seek to foster a future rooted in peace and freed from historical cycles of violence, resentment, and strife. We have a responsibility to nurture the spirit of love in all, but especially our young people, teaching them to practice nonviolence in their own lives, to stand against coercion and intimidation in all forms, and to stand for mutual respect and peace.

Over the centuries, the Inward Light has guided Friends to oppose slavery, to advocate for improving conditions in prisons and abolishing the death penalty, to feed and clothe victims on all sides of wars, to empower the disenfranchised, the outcast, and the stranger. This work continues. As our understanding of God's leadings for us grows, new expressions of our peace witness will emerge, develop, and mature.

Principles and Application

SEEKING HARMONY WITH CREATION

The earth is the LORD's, and everything in it, the world, and all who live in it (Psalm 24:1).

And it would go a great Way to caution and direct People in their Use of the World, that they were better studied and knowing in the Creation of it. For how could Men find the Confidence to abuse it, while they should see the Great Creator look them in the Face, in all and every Part thereof (William Penn)?[18]

The Heart doth love and Reverence God the Creator, and learns to exercise true Justice and Goodness, not only toward all Men, but also toward the brute Creatures...to say we love God, and, at the same Time exercise Cruelty toward the least Creature, is a Contradiction in itself (John Woolman).[19]

Quakers have a long and deep history of respect for the creation of which we are a part. Our wondrous world is a manifestation of the Divine with the power to nourish us physically and spiritually. The ongoing exploitation of the earth's resources threatens the delicate ecological balance that sustains the current web of life. Flowing from our testimonies, Friends' responses take various forms. In 2002, Ohio Valley Yearly Meeting Friends found unity around the principle of sustainability as a basic standard for responsible living.

God calls us, individually and corporately, to examine our lives and take action to walk more lightly on the earth, seeking harmony with creation. Friends are also called to promote systemic changes in government and industry that would heal and protect the earth. With divine assistance, our witness should offer a pattern that would inspire and inform the actions of others.

Principles and Application

SIMPLICITY

> *[Requiring that] we must be all in one dress and one colour: this is a silly poor Gospel. It is more fit for us, to be covered with God's Eternal Spirit, and clothed with his Eternal Light, which leads us and guides us into righteousness (Margaret Fell Fox).*[20]
>
> *Too many of us have too many irons in the fire. We get distracted by the intellectual claim to our interest in a thousand and one good things, and before we know it we are pulled and hauled breathlessly along by an overburdened program of good committees and good undertakings (Thomas R. Kelly).*[21]
>
> *Central to the Friends' testimony on simplicity is the injunction to seek first the kingdom of God (New England Yearly Meeting).*[22]

A life centered on listening to and following the Inward Teacher is characterized by simplicity. This simplicity flows from our direct relationship with God and leads us to maintain humility of spirit and to forego overindulgence, ostentation, and stressful busyness.

The world we live in entices us with distractions. Friends are advised to guard against self-indulgence, extravagance, or obsession with anything else that would lead to neglect of our spiritual lives. Friends recommend simplicity and moderation in our social gatherings, weddings, funerals, and public occasions.

The practice of genuine simplicity is itself simple, and attempts to establish strict norms for simplicity can become distractions. For example, simplicity does not require the rejection of modern technology; indeed, the avoidance of practical technology can lead to the unnecessary complication of one's own life and the lives of others. Simplicity is the natural character of a centered life, not an end in itself. Friends can be tempted to self-righteousness when we reckon our own simplicity to be superior to that of others. Each

Principles and Application

Friend is encouraged to seek divine guidance so that our outward behavior best reflects our inward focus on divine joy.

Practicing simplicity nurtures our spiritual lives, strengthens our interpersonal relationships, and benefits the larger world. By observing and encouraging simple tastes in apparel, furniture, buildings, and manner of living, we do away with unwholesome rivalry. This is helpful for our children who may feel pressured to define themselves and others by their possessions. Teaching our children the basis and practice of simplicity helps them to focus on the fundamentals of respectful relationships. When we curb our impulse to consume, we also strengthen our witness to care for the earth and to act for social justice. Focusing on the Inward Teacher frees us to live simply; living simply frees us to deepen our relationship with God.

Things lawful in themselves may become harmful when used to excess. Friends are advised to observe moderation in everything and to abstain entirely from that which may be the occasion of stumbling for others.

Close Relationships

> *Therefore, as God's chosen people, holy and dearly loved, clothe yourselves with compassion, kindness, humility, gentleness and patience. Bear with each other and forgive whatever grievances you may have against one another. Forgive as the Lord forgave you (Colossians 3:12-13).*

> *See these Quakers, how they love one another (Edward Hicks).*[23]

The fundamental faith of the Religious Society of Friends should be visible in our daily lives. Faithful Friends seek to practice divine love in close relationships with our community of family, friends, and the children under our care. As we experience God's

Principles and Application

love, we grow in love for God and our fellow human beings. Both individuals and monthly meetings have a responsibility to support and nurture spiritually-edifying relationships built on this foundation.

FRIENDSHIP

Deep friendships strengthen us spiritually. They encourage, stretch, challenge, and sustain us. In friendship we respect one another, protect one another's reputation, and honor confidentiality. Good friends minister to one another by listening with an open heart and mind, and by speaking truth with love. Through our experience of friendships across genders, sexualities, classes, generations, faith traditions, races, and ethnicities we move toward establishing the Kingdom of God on earth.

Since the earliest days of our Religious Society, Quakers have been encouraged to know one another in those things that are eternal. Spiritually uplifting friendships require faithfulness to the leadings of the Spirit, not necessarily agreement on every point of faith and practice.

SEXUALITY

Sexuality is a gift from God, regardless of sexual orientation or gender identity. It is a powerful force that can transform life in ways both positive and negative. Mutual love and respect, honesty, and commitment are essential ingredients of a rightly ordered relationship.

Deep respect for that of God in each person requires that our relationships be free of exploitation and abuse as well as subtle manipulation. Abuse of sexuality can have serious, long-term, emotional, physical, and spiritual consequences. Sexuality education for both children and adults should use the best scientific information available. Furthermore, because sexuality can be one of the ways we participate in the love of God, a true understanding of sexuality must also include the spiritual dimension.

Principles and Application

MARRIAGES AND OTHER STEADFAST COMMITMENTS

Our meetings are enlivened and challenged by marriages and other steadfast commitments. Such commitments build spiritual bonds that make themselves felt not only in the home and in the meeting but also in the world. As relationships develop, the partners ideally find richness in sharing on all levels of being: physical, emotional, intellectual, and spiritual.

Some committed partners request marriage under the care of the meeting. (See the **Affirmation of Marriage Equality** on page 18.) Following a discernment process, marriage is solemnized in a meeting for worship, the partners promising with divine assistance to be faithful to each other. We believe that God alone can rightly join partners in marriage, and neither a religious nor a secular official is required to accomplish this. When a Quaker meeting takes a marriage under its care, it witnesses the marriage and makes a serious commitment to support and strengthen that marriage (see **Marriage Procedure** on page 60).

It is the conviction of Friends that marriage is a covenant for life. A lifelong commitment can sustain a marriage through very trying times, forging a deeper and more spiritually mature relationship. Implicit in the marriage promise is the realization that problems and conflicts will arise, and that both partners are committed to making sincere efforts with divine guidance to resolve them. This is not an easy task but a high calling toward which we should strive.

Supporting Families

Meetings have a responsibility to lift up the importance of love, trust, and mutual respect in marriage and other steadfast relationships. As time passes and individuals change, relationships will also change. These changes offer opportunities for spiritual growth and for the deepening of the relationship. Meetings can nurture this process in a variety of ways. This support might range from home visitations to celebrations of anniversaries, holding

Principles and Application

workshops and retreats, or referring couples to resources offered by wider Quaker bodies.

If particular needs or difficulties arise, Friends are advised to hold the couple in prayer and to offer gentle encouragement. It is our experience that a confidential clearness committee offered by the meeting can assist a couple (or an individual) in seeking God's guidance in the relationship (see **Clearness Committees** on page 9). Meetings should be aware of their limitations and be prepared to refer couples to specialized resources beyond the meeting.

Sharing a home

Friends recognize that shared homes include a variety of possible relationships, such as single-parent, two-parent, blended, and multigenerational households, as well as adults living without children. We rejoice and are nourished in homes full of friendliness, refreshment, and peace, where the Light can be felt by those who live there and by all who visit. Such homes reflect caring, trust, and commitment in an atmosphere of good humor and play. The efforts of making a home should be shared with tender regard for the needs and abilities of all members and with appreciation for their unique contributions, recognizing that needs and abilities grow and diminish over the course of each person's life. In the home, our beliefs and practices are tested on a daily basis, and conflicts within families are inevitable. Learning ways to resolve them through openness, honesty, and mutual respect helps strengthen our relationships. Friends are reminded that the guidance of the Light Within is at all times available to lead us into greater love.

Nurturing children

> To watch the spirit of children, to nurture them in Gospel Love, and labour to help them against that which would mar the beauty of their minds, is a debt we owe them; and a faithful performance of our duty not only tends to their lasting benefit and our own peace, but also to render their company agreeable to us (John Woolman).[24]

Principles and Application

Our children are given to us for a time to cherish, to protect, to nurture, and then to salute as they go their separate ways. They too have the light of God within, and a family should be a learning community in which children not only learn skills and values from parents, but in which adults learn new ways of experiencing things and seeing things through young eyes. From their birth on, let us cultivate the habit of dialogue and receptive listening. We should respect their right to grow into their own wholeness, not just the wholeness we may wish for them (Elizabeth Watson).[25]

Every child deserves physical, intellectual, and spiritual nurture. To this end, parents and other adult caregivers must establish themselves as loving and reliable sources of guidance. Caring for children is a life-transforming responsibility, bringing joys, challenges, and experiences of personal and spiritual growth for adult and child. Through good example and consistent teaching, we can counteract many of the negative influences children inevitably encounter. Children are greatly influenced by parents who lead faithful lives, discerning and following the Light Within. Our inward faith is made manifest through practicing simplicity, honesty, nonviolence, service, and love.

To guide our youth toward a life of fulfillment and service, it is essential that Quakers teach their children about creative responses to conflict, the consequences of violent behavior, discernment in sexual activity, the dangers of addiction, and the importance of living in harmony with creation. At the same time, parents and other caregivers should not impose on their children their full range of expectations but rather should have a deep appreciation of who their children are in their own right and support the unfolding of each child's unique gifts. We believe that by nurturing the development of self-worth, self-confidence, and self-discipline, we help children to grow into responsible and compassionate adults. Parents and other caregivers should teach their children about the faith and practice of the Religious Society of Friends, and meetings should

Principles and Application

support children's participation in Quaker youth events and activities. The habit of quiet waiting upon God, both in meeting for worship and in regular family devotion, tends to strengthen and develop the spiritual life of a child.

Special needs and long-term illness

Special needs and long-term illnesses can arise at any time in a person's life and may entail physical, cognitive, social, or psychological challenges. Caring for a child, adult, or aging family member with special needs or a long-term illness can bring unanticipated blessings, but it can also exhaust and isolate the caregiver and can put strain on relationships within the household. Realizing that families may be reluctant to ask for help, Friends should reach out with sensitivity to offer support and nurture to each family in a way appropriate to its unique needs.

Addiction in a home

Addiction to alcohol, drugs, and other substances poses unique challenges that can seriously undermine the health of a household. Friends are encouraged to inform themselves about addictive behavior in order to provide appropriate types of support to addicts and their loved ones. Addiction requires treatment, and the support of an addict requires support for treatment. Even with the best of intentions, providing shelter and sustenance can merely perpetuate the addiction. Meetings should support members who are undertaking the difficult actions required to make recovery possible for members of their households.

Abuse in a home

The exercise of inappropriate power in close relationships can result in physical, psychological, or sexual abuse. In the face of the social isolation often associated with an abusive home, those victimized may feel alone and desperate. Meetings are advised to educate themselves about domestic abuse and to become particularly sensitive to signs of such situations and to be bold in offering

Principles and Application

assistance. Meetings are encouraged to create communities of trust in which those who are being abused can seek the support of the meeting.

Divorce

Friends are cautioned against divorce or separation except under extreme circumstances. Escape from domestic unhappiness through the all too common practice of divorce repudiates an agreement entered into for life, and gives countenance and support to a usage demoralizing to home life. Friends should rather strive, through frequent communication on a deep and honest level, to reconcile differences when they arise. Even when anger and resentment arise, these feelings may be dealt with in constructive ways which contribute to self-knowledge and improved interpersonal relationships.

Although Friends may make every effort to reconcile differences, there are times when close relationships end. Meetings can play a constructive role in these transitions by extending compassionate care to all those involved and responding to that of God in each person. Friends should recognize that children in these situations may be especially in need of the meeting's love and care.

Death

Are you able to contemplate your death and the death of those closest to you? Accepting the fact of death, we are freed to live more fully. In bereavement, give yourself time to grieve. When others mourn, let your love embrace them (Britain Yearly Meeting).[26]

PREPARATION FOR DEATH

An awareness of our mortality may help us to find life richer in the present, to cope better with the deaths of those we love, and to accept death with dignity for ourselves. Friends are encouraged to

Principles and Application

talk openly about death and its meaning for our spiritual lives. Many find that as they face impending death, they are drawn to invite their loved ones into exceptionally frank and open conversations, often leading to emotional healing and forgiveness.

Meetings are encouraged to provide practical education about preparations for death. We can ease the impact of our death on those we love by making certain preparations. Each adult Friend is encouraged to consider making advanced directives, to make a will, and to express preferences regarding organ donations, the disposal of the body, and a memorial meeting. Meetings may wish to keep copies of these documents on file and be prepared to contact relatives in the case of a member's death or other emergency.

BEREAVEMENT

Not even the most careful preparation can alleviate the natural sorrow and grief felt by surviving loved ones. Grieving family and friends will welcome the strength provided by the spiritual, emotional, and practical support of the wider family of Friends. Meetings are advised to recognize that not everyone grieves the death of a loved one in the same way, and Friends are advised to be sensitive to the unique feelings and needs of each grieving person. Friends may be called upon to be compassionate listeners and to help those grieving appreciate how much the gifts of their loved one enriched the lives of others. Friends are advised to be sensitive to grieving survivors during potentially tender times of the year or on particularly tender occasions. All can find support and joy in continuing to celebrate the life of the deceased person while acknowledging the individual's death.

Principles and Application

Stewardship

> *All our rich blessings are but the goods of our kind and gracious Benefactor and are only loaned to us during his good pleasure (Elias Hicks).*[27]

We are called upon to be stewards not only of the Divine Spirit which God has implanted within us, but also of the rich provision which the Creator has made for the sustenance of all life on earth. If we are true followers of Jesus, we must ever be seeking to bring conditions of life in this world into conformity with the purposes of God. It cannot be God's will that vast numbers of our brothers and sisters should pass their lives in surroundings that render difficult the quickening of the Divine Spirit within them. Nor is it sufficient that we should be merely kind and liberal to the poor, for the poverty we seek to relieve may be due in part to unjust conditions, intensified perhaps by our own thoughtless conduct.

Friends should consider how our ways of spending money affect others. We should endeavor to share our advantages and should guard against pursuing modes of life that minister only to our comforts. When we live a life which is attuned to nature and which finds joy and satisfaction in human relationships and personal growth, we will be less dependent on material possessions and more protective of our environment.

Purchasers who buy articles that are useful, well made, and produced under right conditions help to direct industry into channels beneficial to society.

Owners of property, whether in the form of land, stocks, or securities, are counseled to be mindful of the responsibility which their ownership imposes for the management and uses of their property. Investors of money should keep in mind not only the security and rate of interest, but the conditions under which the income is produced.

Principles and Application

WORK IN THE WORLD

Friends in all fields of endeavor are urged to work in the spirit of service, to avoid exploitation of others, and to make our Quaker values visible in the wider world. The highest interests of employers and employees are mutual and interdependent and can be achieved with understanding and cooperation, fairness and goodwill. We urge all to depend on and to be willing to advocate for these principles. When manifest injustice exists in a workplace, each person should conscientiously seek out just means to remedy that injustice.

Those who are employers or supervisors have a responsibility to show respect for each employee as an individual; seeing that everyone's workload is equitable, that each one has reasonable working hours, and that pay rates are consistent with the work performed. In setting wage levels, it is essential that employers consider the needs of employees and their families. Likewise, it is important for workers to maintain a high standard of work quality.

In our relations with corporations as stockholders, Friends should be governed by the same high standards as in our relations with individuals. If the conduct of a corporation is inconsistent with high standards of individual conduct, it is our duty to first call on the corporation to correct the problem. If such protests are unsuccessful, Friends should divest ourselves of stock ownership. It is also inconsistent to work for or to purchase products from such a corporation.

ACCUMULATION OF WEALTH & PAYMENT OF DEBTS

Habits of industry and thrift sometimes degenerate into love for wealth and its accumulation. Clear and accurate accounts are essential to keep Friends aware of their resources and expenditures. Friends are advised to make prompt payment of just debts at the time agreed. It is a moral duty to avoid incurring debts beyond our ability to pay and even when legally discharged of a debt, we should feel that our obligation remains. Friends should be cautious in

Principles and Application

starting a business without requisite capital and experience, or of engaging in risky ventures in order to acquire abnormal profits.

Friends should seek to discern how much of their income or property can be spared, and how it may be wisely distributed for the benefit of others. It should not be a burden but a privilege to be able to contribute when appeals are made to us for the support of our Religious Society and for other worthy causes.

SERVING AS A TRUSTEE

When Friends are in positions of trust, whether as trustee, assignee, treasurer, or other fiduciary capacity in which we are responsible for the administration of the property of others, we should exercise great care to discharge our duties with diligence, good judgment, and the strictest integrity. We must be scrupulous in abiding by the spirit as well as the letter of our promises, contracts, and agreements, in buying and selling, and in all other matters. Any such moneys must be kept strictly apart from our own, with separate accounts maintained, and a careful audit be made yearly of all accounts, including the verification of all investment securities.

ALCOHOL, DRUGS, & TOBACCO

Our bodies are closely responsive to the treatment they receive. They serve us best when they have proper nutrition and healthful living conditions. Friends have traditionally opposed the use of alcohol, tobacco, narcotics, and other addictive drugs for reasons of health and because of the tragedies often resulting from their use. Total abstinence is the clearest witness against the use of harmful substances.

Friends are reminded that their attitudes and examples in the use of alcohol, drugs, and tobacco may be positive educational forces in the lives of others. Let us try by persistent efforts to combat the overwhelming influences of advertising and public license.

Principles and Application

Criticism of varying standards should be tempered by loving appreciation of individual judgment.

RECREATION AND USE OF TIME

Friends understand that each day and each hour is given to us as a gift. We seek patterns of living that enrich and refresh our spiritual and social lives, and involve us in healthy interactions with all of creation. The daily choices we make about use of our time can strengthen or diminish our connections with the Divine Spirit and with one another. Recreation is beneficial and an important part of a balanced life. Friends are advised, however, to examine their use of leisure time and consider whether our recreation is consistent with our understanding of lives centered in truth and love.

For example, Quakers have long borne a testimony against activities such as betting, gambling, and lotteries. We hold a firm belief that such practices are wrong in principle as they promote the false promise of easy, unearned wealth.

Civic Responsibilities

CITIZENSHIP

Friends have a spiritually grounded conception of citizenship and service to their communities, to their nation, and to humanity as a whole. Citizens should encourage their country to cooperate for the betterment of the world. Working to improve the civic, economic, social, and moral condition of one's own country is a truer expression of patriotism than exalting one's own nation at the expense of others, or supporting and justifying its actions irrespective of right or justice.

OBEDIENCE TO LAW & CIVIL DISOBEDIENCE

Our first allegiance is to God, and every Friend should act to influence the making and changing of secular laws so that they may

Principles and Application

more nearly accord with divine love and justice. Friends have a duty to uphold and obey all legal enactments unless they violate the guidance of the Holy Spirit. If conditions arise in which civil law appears to be at variance with divine law, Friends should take prayerful counsel with their communities to discern how they should respond. The spiritual community can sustain and uphold those who are impelled by a higher allegiance to take a difficult stand in deliberately disobeying civil laws. Such action is not taken in disrespect of the law nor with intent to evade its consequences but to live in accordance with the dictates of a higher law. Those who act on the principle of obedience to God must be prepared to suffer for the sake of their convictions.

TREATMENT OF CIVIC OFFENDERS

Enlightened treatment of civic offenders by constructive methods is an historic goal to those who endeavor to follow Quaker principles. Incarceration should be considered only when an individual is a real danger to society. While condemning unrighteous acts, we should seek to have offenders treated as children of God. The end result of incarceration should be rehabilitation and restoration of a right relationship with the community.

Friends are opposed to capital punishment as contrary to divine love. The death penalty is spiritually brutalizing and degrading both to the person executed and to the public mind. It leaves no room for the reformation of the individual nor for revision of the sentence in the event of a miscarriage of justice.

MEETING STRUCTURE, FUNCTION AND PROCEDURES

In addition to meetings for worship, meetings for business have been organized to provide for the orderly care of such matters as are essential to maintaining a religious society. The monthly meeting is where individual membership is recorded. Currently Ohio Valley Yearly Meeting monthly meetings in Ohio and Kentucky belong to Miami Quarterly Meeting and Indiana monthly meetings belong to Whitewater Quarterly Meeting. The two quarterly meetings belong to Ohio Valley Yearly Meeting.

General Business Procedure

The Society of Friends believes that our best decisions are dependent on spiritual discernment. Therefore, it transacts its business by seeking unity under divine guidance rather than by majority vote or even consensus. This means that in our business meetings, each contribution to the discussion is heard in a spirit of prayer. We listen lovingly and respectfully for the voice of God through what each person says.

Presiding clerks are advised to prepare a tentative agenda for business meetings, so that Friends may consider issues in an orderly fashion. When a matter requiring a decision is placed before the meeting, time should be permitted for careful and deliberate consideration. Friends are advised to seek and wait for recognition by the clerk before speaking and to speak succinctly and to the point at hand. Friends are called to seek divine guidance, to exercise mutual forbearance and, when speaking, to refrain from unduly pressing their own views.

When the presiding clerk senses that Friends may be approaching unity around a spiritually grounded judgment, the clerk

Meeting Structure, Function and Procedures

should test the sense of the meeting. If Friends appear to be generally united, the clerk should propose a minute, even if some still wish to speak to the issue. If someone present feels that such a proposed minute does not capture the Light the meeting has been given, they are free to offer an amendment or substitution. While a clerk is working to compose a minute, the meeting is advised to remain in centered worship, holding the clerks in prayer. When it appears that appropriate wording has been found, the presiding clerk asks whether Friends are prepared to approve the minute. When the meeting approves the minute, its final wording is written by the recording clerk and becomes part of the permanent record of the meeting. The minute should be accepted by all members, whether they were present or not, as the best current understanding of the will of God for the meeting.

In some instances, the overwhelming preponderance of Friends may feel united around a proposed course of action, while one or more Friends feel serious hesitations. In such cases, Friends are advised to seek divine guidance about whether they should stand aside or stand in the way. When a Friends stand aside, they faithfully express their hesitations but agree to support the sense of the meeting.

It is important for Friends to bear in mind that standing in the way of a decision on which there is otherwise unity is a privilege granted by the community, not an inherent right of any individual to block an action. When, under a spiritual leading, someone wishes to stand in the way of a proposed action, this means that unity has not been reached. Thus, the proposed action cannot immediately go forward, and Friends will usually continue to labor spiritually about the matter at hand, either at the same meeting for business or in the future. When Friends stand in the way of a decision, they accept the responsibility of continuing to hold the issue in discernment and prayer, are willing to consider that they may be mistaken, and are willing to share a change of conviction, should that occur. On the other hand, there are instances in Friends' experience where the

Meeting Structure, Function and Procedures

faithfulness of a single individual has made it possible for an entire meeting to come to a deeper understanding of the Divine Will for the ultimate way forward.

When a meeting cannot unite on a minute, the old policy remains unchanged or the new business is not taken up (as the case may be) and the subject is dropped for the time being to allow for careful and prayerful contemplation before being considered again.

This method has been followed by Friends since the organization of our Society. It is more than a set of rules; it is an expression of a deep-seated conviction that as religious communities, our meetings should seek to be in spiritual unity with God and each other before proceeding. This has been proven by experience to be both spiritually satisfactory and practically effective. Its use is commended to Friends in conducting both business meetings and committee meetings.

Establishment of Meetings

Friends and seekers who find themselves at a distance from an established monthly meeting may find spiritual sustenance by forming a worship group. These groups often meet in the home of one of the attenders. A worship group is typically not affiliated with any monthly, quarterly, or yearly meeting.

A worship group that desires the company and support of other Friends and wants to be recognized as Quaker as defined by Ohio Valley Yearly Meeting's *Book of Faith and Practice* should request to become a preparative meeting under the care of the nearest Ohio Valley Yearly Meeting monthly meeting. If the monthly meeting agrees to receive this charge, a defined group of monthly meeting members should be selected to assume the responsibility of organizing the preparative meeting and reporting frequently to the monthly meeting.

Meeting Structure, Function and Procedures

Without first becoming a preparative meeting, a worship group could appeal directly to the quarterly meeting to be recognized as a monthly meeting.

A monthly meeting is established by action of its quarterly meeting. The quarterly meeting should investigate and give due consideration to any group requesting to be organized into a new monthly meeting. The quarterly meeting may appoint a committee to render assistance and advice to the group forming a new monthly meeting. This committee should give regular progress reports to the quarterly meeting. Among other considerations, the committee should verify that the new group's members are familiar with the Ohio Valley Yearly Meeting *Book of Faith and Practice*, and that the meeting is organized according to it.

The quarterly meeting may continue its oversight for a year after the establishment of a new monthly meeting, in order to strengthen and aid the members in carrying their new responsibilities.

New monthly meetings are typically formed in one of the four following situations:

The preparative meeting and its monthly meeting agree it is time to recommend that the quarterly meeting recognize the preparative meeting as a new monthly meeting. In this case, it is likely that most of the work of oversight of the new meeting has already been accomplished. Officers and members of the new monthly meeting should be recorded at the quarterly meeting session where the new monthly meeting is approved. Certificates of transfer from the overseeing monthly meeting to the new meeting are not required.

A worship group that appeals directly to the quarterly meeting for recognition as a new monthly meeting places a larger responsibility on the quarterly meeting to investigate that good order is being used among the attenders. The quarterly meeting should appoint a committee for advice and counsel. Officers and new meeting members should be recorded at the quarterly meeting

Meeting Structure, Function and Procedures

session where the new meeting is approved. An attender who is a member in good standing at another monthly meeting must request a certificate of transfer to the new meeting.

If the membership of any monthly meeting should consider it advantageous to separate into two monthly meetings, or to establish a new monthly meeting, they should propose to the quarterly meeting that an approved group of members be set off to constitute the new monthly meeting. Certificates of transfer between the two meetings are not required. The quarterly meeting should appoint a committee to be present at the reorganization to assist in making necessary property adjustments between the two meetings.

A group of Friends who are members of various monthly meetings that desire to organize a new monthly meeting should bring their request before the quarterly meeting with which they wish to be associated. The quarterly meeting which approves the request is directed to appoint a committee to be present and assist, if necessary, in the organization of the new meeting. All members of the new meeting shall request a certificate of transfer from their former monthly meeting to be forwarded to the newly appointed clerk.

A quarterly meeting may be established either upon the initiative of the yearly meeting or upon approval of the yearly meeting of a request from one or more monthly meetings, or from a quarterly meeting that desires to be divided into two quarterly meetings. The yearly meeting, in any case, should appoint a committee to be present and assist if necessary, in the organization.

Discontinuance of Meetings

If it becomes desirable in the judgment of the constituent members of any monthly or preparative meeting to discontinue it or to unite with another, the request should be laid before the meeting to which it reports. The request should be considered and, if

Meeting Structure, Function and Procedures

approved, a committee should be appointed to assist in making the necessary business arrangements, and in the case of the closing of a monthly meeting, to arrange for the proper transfer of individual memberships to another meeting. Information of such action should be forwarded promptly through the proper channels to the yearly meeting.

A preparative meeting should not be discontinued, or suspended, without first consulting the monthly meeting of which it forms a part; a monthly meeting should, in like manner, obtain the approval of the quarterly meeting, and a quarterly meeting should refer a similar request to the yearly meeting.

REVERSION OF PROPERTY

If a preparative meeting ceases to exist, all its records and property shall be transferred and conveyed to the monthly meeting of which it is a part. If a monthly meeting ceases to exist, all its records and property shall be transferred and conveyed to the quarterly meeting of which it is a part. If a quarterly meeting ceases to exist, all its records and property shall be transferred and conveyed to the yearly meeting of which it is a part. If two monthly meetings or two quarterly meetings merge or consolidate, all the property of both shall be held by the merged meeting.

Such transfer and conveyance shall be authorized by an appropriate minute, duly recorded, and the assignment, transfer, and deed of conveyance shall be executed and delivered by the terminating meeting before such meeting is formally laid down or disbanded, or in the case of merged or consolidated meetings, at the time thereof.

In the event that such action is not taken by such meetings before they are laid down, merged, or consolidated, the monthly meeting, the quarterly meeting, or the yearly meeting entitled to receive any such records and property shall be the equitable owner thereof, and shall be entitled forthwith to require the assignment of

Meeting Structure, Function and Procedures

conveyance of the legal title thereto, to be held by such monthly, quarterly, or yearly meeting under and upon the same trusts as the records and property have been theretofore held, if it is practicable that such trusts be carried out; otherwise, upon trusts similar thereto as the successor meeting may determine. No records or meeting property shall be distributed or partitioned among the individual members of a meeting.

If money was invested in such properties or was contributed for the purpose of maintaining meetings and/or burial grounds under the care of Friends, a moral obligation is laid upon us to see that this purpose is served, even though particular meetings may no longer exist. An obligation rests on the receiving meeting to care for properties and burial grounds conveyed to them.

The Executive Committee is directed to assist meetings in placing their meeting properties in suitable trusteeships, if desired. Funds and/or properties may be turned over to the township trustees, historical societies, or other appropriate organizations if it is considered that better care will be obtained in this manner than through the yearly meeting structure.

The Monthly Meeting

The monthly meeting is the fundamental organizational unit of the Society. As the spiritual home of its members and attenders, the monthly meeting provides for their spiritual and temporal needs, fosters the depth of its meetings for worship, supports Spirit-led ministry, and is a source of religious education. It seeks to help all to grow spiritually and to work cooperatively for the strengthening of the Religious Society of Friends. It receives and records the names of members, promotes their spiritual development, extends pastoral care and, when necessary, material aid to its membership. It oversees marriages and memorial meetings. The monthly meeting deals, in a spirit of restoring love, with those who fail to live in accordance with

Meeting Structure, Function and Procedures

our principles and testimonies. It removes names from the membership list if this course seems necessary. It collects the funds required to carry on the work of the meeting, holds titles to property and provides suitable administration of all funds.

When a concern arises to extend the work of the Society of Friends into a new field or to take up specific work under the care of the meeting, it is usually first introduced in a monthly meeting. A monthly meeting is free to undertake any work and to assume any function consistent with our testimonies and not specifically referred to a quarterly meeting or the yearly meeting.

ORGANIZATION

Ohio Valley Yearly Meeting does not impose a specific committee structure on its constituent meetings; rather, each monthly meeting is advised to discern the structure and the qualifications of officers and committees needed to fulfill its functions and to meet its responsibilities.

Officers

Monthly meetings customarily name a suitable person to serve as presiding clerk; this is typically a member. The clerk plays a leadership role in the life of the meeting. The primary duties of the clerk are to conduct all business sessions of the meeting, to see that a full and correct record of all proceedings is kept, and to ensure the accomplishment of the decisions of the meeting on all matters. Assistants to the clerk may be appointed if needed.

Many meetings appoint a recording clerk who makes a written record during monthly business meetings and records decisions that are made. During the business session, the recording clerk reads the minutes in the face of the meeting and the clerk asks for approval of those minutes.

A suitable person shall be named to serve as treasurer to see to the safe and orderly holding and disbursement of funds. The

Meeting Structure, Function and Procedures

treasurer shall report regularly to the meeting and accounts should be audited annually.

Meeting Trustees

Friends recognize that all worldly property belongs to God and that we are merely its stewards. In some cases to meet the requirements of the law, a number of individuals are named as the legally responsible agents for real property or a financial asset. These trustees exist to fulfill the requirements of financial institutions and state and local governments. Although they may be the legal owners of a meeting's property, they are the agents of the meeting and subject to the authority of the business meeting in all matters. To prevent problems, all legal correspondence should be directed to the monthly meeting's mailing address.

Committees

It is the experience of Friends that duly appointed committees are beneficial to the functioning of the monthly meetings by bringing together people with unique skills and experience to address a particular set of issues. Ohio Valley Yearly Meeting leaves the number and definitions of committees to the discernment of its individual constituent monthly meetings. In some cases, committees directly carry out specific tasks; in others, committees season proposals for presentation and consideration at a monthly meeting for business. In especially small meetings, the entire meeting community frequently attends to many or all of its responsibilities.

Most often, a Nominating Committee is named to bring forward the names of members or attenders to serve the meeting for clearly defined terms. In doing their work, the Nominating Committee seeks a balance of Friends who already have appropriate gifts and skills for each office and committee, while keeping in mind the opportunity for Friends to grow once they have been appointed to a particular role. All nominations are subject to approval at meeting for business.

Meeting Structure, Function and Procedures

The work of committees is facilitated by the appointment of a committee clerk, who is responsible for calling and clerking committee meetings and presenting committee reports to the monthly meeting. In some meetings, the committee clerks are approved by the monthly meeting; other meetings appoint conveners who are responsible simply for calling an initial committee meeting, at which committee members discern who should serve as committee clerk.

Friends are advised to hold committee meetings in the manner of Friends meetings for business. This includes opening with a period of centering worship, striving to listen with an open heart and mind for divine guidance, loving and respectful treatment of all participants when disagreements arise, and searching for unity in the Spirit rather than voting. Committees are helped by the practice of recording minutes that are read and approved in the face of the committee. Standing committees meet on a regular basis, generally once a month.

In addition to its value to the meeting, service on meeting committees is an important opportunity for spiritual growth and the deepening of Friendly bonds within the meeting as a whole. Committee members are also called to provide spiritual support to one another in their often challenging work.

FOSTERING THE MEETING FOR WORSHIP

Fostering the right order and spiritual depth of meeting for worship must be done in humility of spirit – confident that the power of God working in us will yield greater depth in worship and vocal ministry, opening new avenues of usefulness. Meetings are urged to appoint a committee (often called the Committee for Ministry and Counsel) to focus on the spiritual well-being of the meeting as a community and, in particular for the meeting for worship.

Meeting Structure, Function and Procedures

This committee should offer encouragement, support, advice, and useful feedback to those who are led to speak. The committee should be mindful that there are differences in ability, training, fluency of expression, and power of interpretation. Having tested an urge to speak and found it a genuine leading, no one should hesitate because of inexperience. The spirit of a message is more than its form and the example of one struggling to be faithful in a difficult task may be more helpful than the most polished address.

Meeting for worship is a balance between silence and vocal ministry. Words are important, as is quietly waiting for direct communion with God. This is the basis on which our meetings are held. When this stillness is unduly limited by an excess of vocal expression, this committee is tasked with calling attention to our need for silent waiting during worship. This committee may also be called on to labor with a member or attender who habitually speaks unacceptably, providing the speaker with prompt and loving counsel. Likewise, when there are prolonged periods of silence, the committee may need to find ways to encourage Friends to respond when they feel divine promptings to speak.

Members and attenders who are troubled by the quality of the meeting for worship or the content of a message are urged to bring these concerns to this committee.

PASTORAL CARE

There are times when some members and their families need added consideration and compassion. This may result from changes in material circumstances, whether joyous events, such as the birth of a child, or adverse ones, such as illness or the loss of a job. At other times, a member or attender may be in the midst of an emotional or spiritual struggle. The meeting should be ready to provide help or assistance, to whatever extent it is able. Such work can be an overwhelming burden for individuals in the meeting to carry. A committee for pastoral care can provide a safe and confidential place to bring concerns. The committee should have a

Meeting Structure, Function and Procedures

variety of skills and proficiencies from Friends who feel a special responsibility for the welfare of members and attenders. These Friends are charged with encouraging all members and attenders to faithful performance of their duties. This will require that committee members become acquainted with the whole meeting community and keep informed about various needs for encouragement or assistance.

Sometimes, a commitment to Quaker principles results in some form of hardship. Meetings should be sensitive to the conditions of their membership and prepared to release individuals to witness in whatever manner they feel called. This may mean taking on the care of a family, giving public support to the witness, or simply helping the individual to clarify priorities. Oversight of such situations may fall to the committee charged with pastoral care or it may be the charge of a specially appointed Clearness Committee (see **Clearness Committees** on page 9). When an individual requests a Clearness Committee, our usual practice is for the committee charged with pastoral care to assume responsibility for naming the committee in consultation with the individual concerned.

In addition to encouraging faithful action, the meeting needs to be alert to instances of failure. If a member repeatedly disregards Friends' principles, the meeting's standards of conduct, or the obligations of membership, a designated committee will counsel that member in a spirit of loving concern, endeavoring to effect a change in the individual's conduct and reconciliation with the meeting. If these efforts are unsuccessful, the committee may be obligated to bring the matter to the attention of the monthly meeting with a report of their efforts. It is never acceptable for the committee to act alone in excluding an individual from attendance or participation in the monthly meeting.

Responsibility for pastoral care may be assigned to the committee charged with fostering the depth of worship or it may be the primary charge of a separate committee. It is important that both

Meeting Structure, Function and Procedures

sets of responsibilities receive adequate attention. In the case of two separate committees, there needs to be a clear understanding of the division of labor between the committees, and Friends have found it useful for the two committees to hold joint meetings at least once a year.

RELIGIOUS EDUCATION

Religious education helps to establish and foster right relationships with God, with other people, and with all of creation. For both children and adults, such opportunities encourage renewed commitment to Friends principles and can support a spiritually grounded way of living. To meet these needs and to support a lifetime of Quaker learning, each meeting is encouraged to provide study of the Bible, Quaker history, and the beliefs and values of the Religious Society of Friends.

Education of Children, Adolescents, and Young Adults

In addition to religious education, meetings have a responsibility for the schooling of their young people. Meetings should exercise care that all their children, adolescents, and young adults receive the education that they need. For some, education at a Friends school or college may be most appropriate. When possible, meetings should help with the costs of educational experiences.

OUTREACH

When we experience the creative energy and power of God in our lives, then we too will want to share it and look for ways to invite visitors or inquirers to join with us. This requires us to make our meetings and our witness visible to the wider world. As we reach out to seekers, our overall goal should be to clearly present who we are and what we believe, interpreting the Quaker way with both openness and integrity, remembering that inquirers and newcomers may be drawn to the Religious Society of Friends for a variety of reasons. When we organize or participate in events and activities that reflect our testimonies, we should share the spiritual basis of our

Meeting Structure, Function and Procedures

actions. Our goal is to provide a warm and welcoming spiritual community that invites newcomers fully into the life of the meeting.

STATE OF THE MEETING REPORT

An annual State of the Meeting Report is intended to describe the meeting's spiritual condition and needs, together with an account of its own efforts to meet those needs. These reports are typically drafted by the committee charged with the care of the meeting for worship and presented to monthly meeting for business for consideration and final approval. The State of the Meeting report is then presented in a timely manner to the appropriate quarterly meeting and forwarded to the yearly meeting in advance of annual sessions. The committee charged with drafting a State of the Meeting report may be aided in its deliberations by considering some or all of the following:

1. What is the general spiritual condition of your meetings for worship and business?
2. Does your meeting assemble quietly and reverently for worship?
3. Do most of your resident members attend and find the meetings for worship and business valuable?
4. Do members assist according to their ability in making meetings spiritually profitable?
5. Is the vocal ministry helpful to the meeting? What steps have been taken to deepen the vocal ministry?
6. Do Friends feel a lack of vocal ministry when little or none exists? How do you think this lack can be met?
7. Are you careful to protect your meeting for worship from too much speaking or irrelevant addresses lacking spiritual value?
8. How do you keep Friends' spiritual principles clearly before your members and attenders?

Meeting Structure, Function and Procedures

9. What is the spiritual condition of the meeting community? Are there adequate opportunities for members and attenders to come to know each other in things that are eternal?
10. What conditions and activities have affected the life of your meeting in the past year?
11. How do your members and the meeting as a whole exercise stewardship for the things God has entrusted to you?
12. What are the most pressing needs which you feel for the meeting?

It is important to avoid submitting a list of events and activities undertaken over the course of the year as a State of the Meeting report. However, reflection on the spiritual benefits or hazards associated with a particular event or activity can in some cases be useful in helping ourselves and others understand the spiritual state of a monthly meeting.

The OVYM Religious Nurture and Education Committee reviews the State of the Meeting Reports, which helps inform the Yearly Meeting's State of Society Report. The State of the Meeting Reports are published every year in the Yearly Meeting Minute Book.

MEMBERSHIP

Membership in the Religious Society of Friends...is both a privilege and a responsibility. Ideally, it is the outward sign of an inner experience of the living God and of unity with the other members of a living body (New England Yearly Meeting).[28]

Membership expresses a commitment to the Religious Society of Friends, founded on the belief that God is actively guiding the individual and the community of faith. Becoming a member expresses outwardly an inward leading toward spiritual enlightenment and growth. When a meeting accepts a person into membership, the meeting and the new member enter into a long-term, spiritually-based covenant relationship.

Meeting Structure, Function and Procedures

Membership entails several responsibilities including bearing faithful testimony to the guiding principles of the Religious Society of Friends and giving of one's energy, time, and financial resources, as one is able. Members are expected to faithfully attend meetings for worship and for business, and are encouraged to participate in quarterly and yearly meeting activities. Members should be willing to enter into a process of loving discernment with the meeting to seek where their gifts and talents can be most helpful. Such service may include pastoral care, religious education, witness to the broader community, or involvement in the broader Quaker world.

Attenders

There are those who manifest a continuing interest in the life of the meeting but have not entered into formal membership. Friends welcome the participation of such active attenders in the activities of the meeting, offer them guidance and instruction in Quakerism, and nurture their spiritual growth. Active attenders, nourished through their involvement with the meeting, familiar with and enriched by Friends' basic beliefs and practices, and willing to undertake greater responsibilities within the meeting are encouraged to apply for membership.

Preparation for Membership

Friends consider membership to be a serious relationship to be entered into after careful discernment. It is generally recommended that an individual considering application for membership attend meetings for worship and for business regularly, seek service on a meeting committee, and undertake a personal study of Quaker faith and practice. Prospective applicants for membership need not delay application fearing they have not yet attained a particular level of spirituality. Becoming a member is intended to mark the beginning of a long-term commitment to a way of life, not its ultimate completion.

Meeting Structure, Function and Procedures

Membership Application Process

Those who desire to become members of the Religious Society of Friends should apply to the monthly meeting they attend by submitting a letter stating this request to the clerk of the Committee for Ministry and Counsel. The committee will then appoint a clearness committee to meet with the applicant (see **Clearness Committees** on page 9). The clearness committee should include one or more members of the Committee for Ministry and Counsel and may include other seasoned members of the meeting. The members of the committee will hold worshipful discussions with the applicant as often and for as long as necessary for all to reach unity regarding the rightness of the relationship and the readiness of the applicant for membership. During the clearness committee's deliberations, applications for membership should generally be treated as confidential.

After meeting with the candidate, the clearness committee reports its findings to the Committee for Ministry and Counsel. When clearness to move forward with an application is reached, the Committee for Ministry and Counsel should report the recommendation for membership to the next regularly appointed monthly meeting for business. The committee's report is to be recorded in a minute, but no action on the application is to be taken at that meeting for business. At this time Friends are encouraged to get to know the applicant if they have not done so earlier, and Friends who have questions or reservations about the applicant should explore these with the Committee for Ministry and Counsel. At the following regular monthly meeting for business, Friends should consider the application for membership and, if prepared to do so, should approve it, recording the action in a minute. The individual thereby becomes a member of the monthly meeting and of the quarterly and yearly meetings of which the monthly meeting is a constituent member. It is customary for Friends to appoint a committee to welcome the individual into membership.

Meeting Structure, Function and Procedures

If it becomes clear during the application process to the applicant, to the Clearness Committee, or to both that membership is not advisable or not advisable at this time, the application may be withdrawn. Friends are advised to respond lovingly to such applications, encouraging the applicant to continue attendance and participation in the life of the meeting. Those whose applications are withdrawn may be led to reapply for membership at a later time. Membership itself is not as important as the spiritual growth of the prospective member.

Youth Membership

Quaker communities rest on a principle of equality and on the worth of every individual. We value and welcome the young people who attend our meetings and participate in the lives of our communities. At the same time, our faith rests on deep personal and individual experience, and membership in the Religious Society of Friends and in a particular monthly meeting calls for a serious commitment. One person cannot make this commitment for another, and a caregiver cannot make this commitment for a young child. In order to accommodate both of these spiritual insights, Ohio Valley Yearly Meeting presents the following procedures as a model to consider. These procedures recognize both youth membership and adult membership and outline a process for transition to adult membership. Regardless of a Friend's age, the term youth membership as used here is understood as membership requested by another on that Friend's behalf, while the term adult membership is understood as membership requested by that Friend directly.

Members who are parents or individuals with parental responsibility who intend to bring up a child in accordance with Friends' faith and practice may request youth membership for the child. Monthly meetings may accept minor children as youth members at the request of one or both of their parents or guardians. The Committee for Ministry and Counsel should approach members who are new parents or parents requesting transfer of membership

Meeting Structure, Function and Procedures

and ask if they would like to request youth membership for their children. Likewise, the membership clearness process for new members who are parents should include the children in the discussion of membership. When the monthly meeting accepts a child into youth membership, the child will also be considered a youth member of the relevant quarterly meeting and of Ohio Valley Yearly Meeting.

Children must ultimately make their own decision about adult membership. Youth members may request transition to adult membership at any time they feel ready to do so, by writing a simple letter to the Committee for Ministry and Counsel. Ohio Valley Yearly Meeting recommends that monthly meetings appoint membership clearness committees for youth members seeking transition to adult membership, following the same procedures set forth above for new membership.

To help prepare children for making this decision, the meeting should teach children about the meaning and responsibilities of membership. This process includes teaching children how to enter into waiting worship and how to participate in the Spirit-led Quaker business process, giving them opportunities to accept responsibilities such as participation on committees as they are able, and encouraging them to participate in youth groups associated with quarterly meetings, Ohio Valley Yearly Meeting, and Friends General Conference.

When parents or other adult Friends sense that a young person may be ready for adult membership, they should encourage the youth member to consider taking this step. The Committee for Ministry and Counsel should send a letter to each youth member around age 16, expressing appreciation for the young person's gifts and growing spiritual maturity, and encouraging them to consider whether the time is right to request adult membership. The Committee for Ministry and Counsel should continue to send letters to the youth member every two or three years between the ages of

Meeting Structure, Function and Procedures

16 and 25. The youth member should be asked to make a decision by his or her 25th birthday.

If a youth member has not requested adult membership by age 25, youth membership status ends, and the monthly meeting will minute that action. Should a youth members of any age inform the meeting that they do not wish to remain members of the Religious Society of Friends, the Committee for Ministry and Counsel is advised to seek discernment regarding the appropriate course of action in each individual case. However, if a youth member is clear about resignation, the monthly meeting will minute that the individual's youth membership has ended. These young people should be warmly assured that they are welcome to continue as active attenders, that they may at any time request membership, and that the meeting will continue to support them with loving care.

Friends recognize that monthly meetings may discern alternative procedures concerning membership of children. Whatever procedures are adopted should reflect Friends' sense of loving concern and responsibility for children, as well as our belief in the value of raising children as part of a spiritual community.

Dual Membership

Membership is a commitment to participate in a particular community of Friends, and full participation in two religious bodies at once is usually impractical. Dual membership is generally discouraged. Except in unusual circumstances, a member of Ohio Valley Yearly Meeting belongs to a particular monthly meeting and should not hold full membership in another religious body, including another monthly meeting.

Sojourning Membership

When Friends find themselves temporarily residing away from their home meeting, they may wish to be released from most of the usual responsibilities of membership in the home meeting and be willing to take on such responsibilities in their new location. Such

Meeting Structure, Function and Procedures

Friends may ask their home meeting to issue a sojourning minute, which is then conveyed to the presiding clerk of the new meeting. Upon acceptance of the Friend as a sojourning member, the presiding clerk of the new meeting will inform the clerk of the home meeting. Sojourning members are considered fully participating members and may serve the new meeting in whatever ways are fitting. However, the primary financial responsibility of these members will remain with their home meeting, and they will also be counted in their home meeting's statistical report. Sojourning status ends when the sojourner leaves the new meeting and the presiding clerk of the new meeting so notifies the home meeting. Friends who find that their stay is longer than two years should seriously consider transferring their membership.

Transfer of Membership

It is recommended that members who move away from their monthly meeting seek a new meeting where they can assume full responsibilities of membership. When such a meeting is found, the Friend will ask the home meeting to issue a certificate of transfer. Upon verifying that the applicant is a member, the home meeting's Committee for Ministry and Counsel brings the request before the monthly meeting for approval. Once issued, the certificate of transfer is conveyed to the presiding clerk of the new monthly meeting, where it should be referred to the Committee for Ministry and Counsel for review. When prepared to do so, the Committee for Ministry and Counsel brings forward the request to the business meeting. Upon approval, the Friend is recorded as a member of the new meeting, and the old meeting is notified of this action. Until this is done, the Friend remains a member of the old meeting. The new monthly meeting should appoint one or more Friends to welcome the transferred member.

TERMINATION OF MEMBERSHIP

Membership in the Religious Society of Friends can be terminated in cases of (a) resignation (b) loss of interest in

Meeting Structure, Function and Procedures

membership or (c) disownment, each of which is explained below. Termination of membership becomes effective only when a record to this effect is made in the minutes of the monthly meeting of which that person is a member. One whose membership has been discontinued and who desires to be reinstated may be received into membership in accordance with the procedure for admitting new members.

Resignation

A member wishing to resign from membership should address a letter of resignation to the presiding clerk of the monthly meeting. The clerk should refer the letter to the Committee for Ministry and Counsel. Normally, a resignation should not be accepted until after a visit (or exchange of correspondence) to inquire sensitively into the matter. If the member does not reconsider, the Committee for Ministry and Counsel should report this to the meeting, and the meeting should release that Friend from membership. The clerk should inform the former member in writing of the action.

Loss of Interest

Membership entails participation in the life of one's monthly meeting as a spiritual community. Meetings and their members share a mutual commitment to each other's spiritual wellbeing. When Friends become concerned about a member who has not attended meeting for worship or communicated with the meeting, the Committee for Ministry and Counsel should contact the individual, expressing the meeting's care and loving concern. Friends should seek through the grace of God and the spirit of divine love to restore this Friend to regular fellowship with the community, and to provide assistance and support, if possible. In some cases, it may be necessary for Friends to approach the individual repeatedly. If, after sincere and diligent effort, restoration of interest in the meeting is unsuccessful, the monthly meeting may adopt a minute removing the member from membership. The meeting should, if possible, inform the individual of this action.

Meeting Structure, Function and Procedures

Disownment

A member whose conduct or publicly expressed views repeatedly undermine Friends' testimonies should be labored with lovingly and patiently for as long as there is reasonable hope of restoring unity with the fellowship. No judgment should be placed hastily or in the spirit of condemnation. Monthly meetings, however, may decide it is necessary to record a minute of disunity with such a person's actions.

In rare and exceptional circumstances, the meeting also has the authority to terminate a person's membership through disownment. This process begins when the Committee for Ministry and Counsel brings forward to the monthly business meeting a minute justifying a recommendation of disownment. If the business meeting agrees to proceed with the recommendation, the member should be promptly notified of the charges in writing and should be given an opportunity to present the member's case to the meeting at a called meeting for business devoted exclusively to this matter.

The monthly meeting should assure itself that all possible steps to aid the member's return to unity with the meeting have been taken, remembering that all persons are subject to error, and that love and forgiveness may restore unity. After careful consideration, but without undue delay, the meeting may approve a minute terminating membership. In that case, a copy of the minute should be delivered to the individual along with notification of the right to appeal. A disowned person is released from the rights and responsibilities of membership; however, disownment does not mean a severing of all relationship between the meeting and the disowned person. Friends are encouraged to treat this person with loving kindness.

Appeals

If a disowned person believes that the monthly meeting has rendered an unjust judgment, that person may appeal to the quarterly meeting. The individual making the appeal should promptly notify

Meeting Structure, Function and Procedures

the presiding clerks of the quarterly meeting and the monthly meeting. The quarterly meeting is then to refer the case to a suitable committee, excluding Friends from the monthly meeting involved. The monthly meeting should appoint a committee to represent it in the appeals process and should provide the quarterly meeting's appeals committee with copies of all minutes having a bearing on the case. The appeals committee should meet with both parties, prayerfully consider the case, and report its recommendation to the following quarterly business meeting. The quarterly meeting shall consider the recommendation, confirm or reverse the original judgment, or return the case to the monthly meeting for further consideration. Care should be taken to inform the person making the appeal and the monthly meeting of the decision, either of which, if dissatisfied, may appeal to the yearly meeting for further hearing.

In the case of such an appeal, the yearly meeting shall in like manner refer the appeal to a suitable committee, excluding Friends from the quarterly meeting involved. This committee shall meet with the individual and representatives from the monthly meeting and the quarterly meeting, have access to all relevant minutes, and make a recommendation to the yearly meeting. The yearly meeting will then uphold or reverse the original decision, and yearly meeting's decision will be final. At either level of appeal, parties may agree to accept the judgment of the appeals committee and not bring the matter before the entire meeting body.

MARRIAGE PROCEDURE

(See also **Marriages and Other Steadfast Commitments** on page 26.)

The covenant of marriage is solemn in its obligation, fundamental in its social significance, and should be lifelong in its duration. When a monthly meeting assumes oversight of a marriage, it makes an enduring commitment to support and strengthen that marriage. The meeting is asked not only to approve the wedding and see it performed in good order, but also to care for and share in the

Meeting Structure, Function and Procedures

marriage, and help in its success with advice and counsel. Friends consider that asking a monthly meeting to take a marriage under its care places responsibilities on both the couple and the meeting.

For its proper accomplishment under the care of our Society, the following procedure is recommended:

The couple proposing marriage should communicate their intentions to the monthly meeting under whose care the wedding will be held by writing a letter, signed by them both, requesting the meeting's approval for marriage.

The Committee for Ministry and Counsel will then name a clearness committee to meet with the couple. When one or both members of the couple is a member of another religious body, an invitation may be extended to that community to participate in the clearness process.

The clearness committee will meet one or more times with the couple to determine their readiness for marriage. The couple is part of the committee and participates in this discernment.

If the clearness committee recommends approval, this is presented to the next monthly meeting for business for its approval. The monthly meeting should approve that the marriage be carried out.

Two or more Friends are appointed by the monthly meeting to have care and oversight of the wedding. Proposed names for the Marriage Oversight Committee may be brought forward by the couple.

The wedding is held under the care of the monthly meeting.

This Marriage Oversight Committee shall report to the next monthly meeting concerning the following: the observance of good order in the wedding, delivery of the marriage certificate or duplicate to the recorder of the monthly meeting for recording, compliance

Meeting Structure, Function and Procedures

with legal requirements, and the names assumed or retained by the couple.

Clearness Committee for Marriage

(See also **Clearness Committees** on page 9.)

The clearness committee for a proposed marriage was originally intended to determine if the couple was clear of any obstacles to marriage. It inquired into the character and obligations of the couple, compliance with the provisions of state laws, and to see that the rights and feelings of any children were taken into account. Contemporary committees assume a broader role: searching deeply into the relationship of the couple and helping them determine their readiness for the commitments of marriage. If one or both partners has been divorced, the committee should determine that the special challenges of remarriage have been carefully considered.

The committee should help the couple explore questions and areas of their relationship that they perhaps have not considered. Such a procedure is intended to enable the couple to understand as fully as possible the new relationship into which they may enter, as well as to identify their own expectations and capabilities.

The committee obviously cannot present all of the possibilities of a marriage to a couple, nor can all potential problems be anticipated, but deep searching in a spirit of love and tender seeking can help the couple find a better understanding of the roles and responsibilities of marriage.

Marriage of Two Non-Members

When two non-members request oversight of their marriage, the Committee for Ministry and Counsel should inquire into the reasons for the request. If the committee approves the meeting's assuming the responsibility, they shall bring their recommendation to monthly meeting for business. If the monthly meeting agrees to the oversight of the marriage, a clearness committee is appointed. This Committee

Meeting Structure, Function and Procedures

shall proceed in the manner of Friends, with the same care as when one or both parties are members of the Society of Friends.

Marriage Ceremony

When a marriage has been authorized and the meeting is gathered at which it is to be accomplished, it is advised that a period of silent worship be observed, during which the parties to the marriage should rise, and taking each other by the hand, each should declare in words to this effect: "In the presence of God and before these, our friends, I take (you/thee), _____, to be my (husband/wife/spouse), promising, with divine assistance, to be unto (you/thee) a loving and faithful (husband/wife/spouse), as long as we both shall live."

After these declarations, the marriage certificate should be signed by the couple and read by someone from the Marriage Oversight Committee. Worship should continue and the meeting closed by the Marriage Oversight Committee.

Changes may take place in wedding forms and procedures with the approval of the Marriage Oversight Committee. The marriage certificate may be modified, and the wedding may be planned to suit the needs of the couple.

Form of Certificate

The form of the certificate may follow one of these examples:

Traditional Certificate Example:

Whereas, A.B, of _____, child of C.B. and D.B., of _____, and E.F., child of G.F. and H.F., of _____, having declared their intentions of marriage to each other to _____ Monthly Meeting of the Religious Society of Friends, held at _____, according to the good order used among Friends, their proposed marriage was approved by that Meeting.

Now this is to certify to whom it may concern, that for the accomplishment of their intentions, this ___ day of the ___

Meeting Structure, Function and Procedures

month, in the year of our Lord _____, during an appointed Meeting for Worship, A.B. and E.F., appeared in a meeting of the Religious Society of Friends, held at _____; and taking one another by the hand, did on this solemn occasion declare that they took each other in marriage, promising with Divine assistance to be loving and faithful spouses to one another, as long as they both shall live. And, moreover, they, A.B. and E.F. did, as a further confirmation thereof, then and there, to these present set their hands.

We, whose names are also signed below, being present at the said marriage, have, as witnesses thereunto, set our hands the day and year above written.

Contemporary Certificate Example:

R.B. of ___, child of F.W.B. and V.H.B. of ___, and C.S. of ___, child of T.W.S. and R.G.S. of ___, declared their intention to marry each other, to the ___ Monthly Meeting of the Religious Society of Friends. Their proposed marriage was approved by that Meeting.

On the ___ day of the ___ month of the year ___, during an appointed Meeting for Worship, R.B. and C.S. declared that they took one another in marriage, promising with Divine assistance to be loving and faithful spouses to one another as long as they both shall live.

R. and C. in an outward and visible confirmation of the marriage then signed this certificate.

We who have signed this certificate have witnessed this marriage while worshipping together.

MEETING RECORDS

All meetings for business should keep full and correct records of their transactions in convenient form for reference. An accurate record of the membership of each monthly meeting should be kept

Meeting Structure, Function and Procedures

which should include all births, marriages, removals, and deaths occurring among members. (See **Annual Statistical Report** on page 73.)

Ohio Valley Yearly Meeting has arranged for storing the yearly meeting's records and those of its subordinate meetings in the facilities of the Quaker Collection housed in the Wilmington College Library. The following records should be deposited as soon as they are no longer needed for the business of the meeting, which will normally be within three to five years:

1. Minutes of the meetings.
2. Minutes of the preparative meetings, the Committee for Ministry and Counsel, other committees, and the like.
3. Membership, statistical, marriage and burial records.
4. Official correspondence of the meetings.
5. Deeds or other similar documents relating to any property held by the meeting.
6. Newsletters or bulletins.
7. Any other committee records.
8. The treasurer's records.
9. Photographs, slides, tapes, etc. of meeting events.
10. Correspondence to or from the meeting or the meeting clerk, except routine printed communications such as annual reports from Friends organizations.

These records will remain available for withdrawal and for additions to or updating of the records upon presentation to the Quaker Collection Curator of a letter of authorization from the clerk of the meeting making the deposit or its successor. Thus, meetings are encouraged to store records in the fire-resistant vault at Wilmington College even if the records may be needed at some time in the future.

Meeting Structure, Function and Procedures

A recorder or statistician may be appointed to carry out these duties; each meeting should furnish suitable books and provide proper places in which to preserve the records.

RECORDED MINISTERS

Some monthly meetings record gifts of ministry. Among the many possible avenues are travelling in the ministry, speaking publicly, teaching, or other service. Recording a Friend's gifts of ministry implies that the individual has submitted to God's will and to the discernment of their faith community. Recorded ministers accept the sacred responsibility to continue to exercise the gift as God intended with the aid and support of their faith community. The process of recording gifts of ministry begins when a monthly meeting forms a clearness committee for the purpose of determining whether or not there is a call to ministry (see **Clearness Committees** on page 9).

A recorded minister should meet at least annually with a support committee associated with the monthly meeting for ongoing clearness and nurture, and to help discern whether the call to ministry continues or if the recording should be laid down.

Even when a meeting does not formally record gifts of ministry, it remains the responsibility of the meeting to nurture and support all members' gifts.

ECCLESIASTICAL ENDORSEMENT

Some Friends may request an ecclesiastical endorsement as a professional qualification. In such cases, it is the responsibility of the monthly meeting to review the professional requirements and the Friend's qualifications. When a meeting unites in an ecclesiastical endorsement, it has a responsibility to provide ongoing nurture and support of the Friend, and to regularly review and renew the endorsement.

Meeting Structure, Function and Procedures

In addition to the meeting reviewing professional requirements and the Friend's qualifications, the meeting should also discern with them whether they uphold Quaker values in their work, and whether the Friend is a member and intends to continue to remain connected to the meeting.

INTERVISITATION

The membership of a meeting may be stimulated to greater faithfulness by the visits of members of other meetings, who often bring valuable spiritual insights. It may also be helpful to a monthly meeting if its members, individually or in groups, visit other Friends' meetings for worship.

Letter of Introduction

A member of the monthly meeting may have occasion to travel and may wish to make contact with other members of the Society of Friends. The monthly meeting clerk may write a letter of introduction stating that the person is a member in good standing. The letter may also convey love from the meeting to those visited by the traveler. This letter may be presented by the traveler to those Friends visited.

Traveling Minute

When Friends feel called to religious service beyond their own monthly meeting, or to visit the families therein, they should first lay the matter before their monthly meeting, stating so far as can be foreseen, the whole nature of the proposed service. If the monthly meeting feels free to unite with the concern, it shall make a minute to that effect and furnish the Friends with a copy thereof.

When the service is directed outside of the Friend's own quarterly meeting or yearly meeting, the quarterly meeting or yearly meeting (or its Executive Committee) should be informed of the concern. If the quarterly meeting or yearly meeting approves, it should endorse the monthly meeting's minute, or issue a minute by its own clerks, indicating its approval.

Meeting Structure, Function and Procedures

After the accomplishment of such services, the meetings which have granted the traveling minutes should be promptly notified and their documents returned to them without delay. Friends returning minutes should report on their visits for the information and encouragement of the meetings which have supported them in their concerns.

Any meeting which grants minutes for travel should take care that, as far as possible, the service is not hindered for lack of sufficient funds.

Clerks of meetings visited should recognize and endorse the traveling minute carried by a visiting Friend.

MEETING FUNDS

Meetings should raise funds sufficient to meet their responsibilities, to care for their property, and to provide for their obligations to the quarterly and yearly meetings.

The Ohio Valley Yearly Meeting Budget and Finance Committee determines the proportionate share of the yearly meeting budget for each local meeting and notify each meeting.

INCORPORATION

It is recommended that all meetings that own real property should incorporate. In documents of incorporation, the monthly meeting's address should be provided to the state government and not that of an individual trustee. As required by each state, a certificate of continued existence may need to be filed periodically. To avoid lapse resulting from the death of trustees holding title to meeting properties and trusts, it is advised that such titles and trusts be held by corporations when practicable. The Executive Committee will advise with any meeting contemplating incorporation.

Meeting Structure, Function and Procedures

MEETING TRUSTS & PROPERTY TITLES

Monthly and preparative meetings, as well as quarterly and yearly meetings, are advised to require annual reports of the income, disbursements, and of the investment of the principal of all trusts, including the status of titles for meeting properties, and burial grounds. Trustees' records must maintain accurate statements of the terms of all trusts held for the benefit of the meeting or of the Religious Society of Friends at large.

Business meetings are cautioned to see that timely care is taken for the renewal of trusts. They are exhorted to be diligent and particular as to the careful investment of trust funds. The assistance of the Executive Committee may be sought if difficulties arise.

BURIAL GROUNDS

Two or more Friends should be appointed to have the care of a meeting's burial grounds and see that interments are made in accordance with the practices approved by the meeting which owns the grounds.

Careful marking of all graves for purposes of identification should be practiced and records thereof kept. Our principles of moderation and simplicity should be strictly observed in marking graves.

Quarterly Meeting

The quarterly meeting is designed to bring together for inspiration and counsel a larger group, and to consider more varied interests than any single meeting embraces. It is composed of constituent monthly meetings, each of which shall appoint one or more representatives to attend it.

Meeting Structure, Function and Procedures

Its form of organization should be similar to that of the monthly meeting. It is to receive and forward reports from monthly meetings to the yearly meeting. It may hold property and trusts, and appoint for specific services committees over which it shall have original and final jurisdiction. Its most helpful function should be to aid and encourage the monthly meetings composing it to greater interest and service, and to give its members an increasing vision of the truth. It should be diligent in seeking opportunities to gather together groups which may be organized into meetings, and should always be ready to help monthly meetings whenever they ask for advice or assistance.

Yearly Meeting

The yearly meeting is composed of its constituent quarterly meetings and monthly meetings. Each monthly meeting appoints representatives to attend sessions of the yearly meeting. These representatives perform whatever duties the yearly meeting or the meeting which appoints them may assign. It is advised that they make reports to their respective monthly meetings of important action taken by the yearly meeting. All members of constituent monthly meetings are also members of the yearly meeting and have the same privileges as the representatives. The yearly meeting appoints necessary officers, including presiding clerk, assistant presiding clerk, recording clerk, treasurer, and statistician.

The yearly meeting may organize its work through the appointment of committees necessary for effectively carrying out its concerns. It is cautioned against becoming over-organized and thus expending energy in maintaining a mechanical system which should be conserved for the advancement of truth.

It will annually determine a budget necessary for its expenses and inform each monthly meeting a proportional share amount based on total membership.

Meeting Structure, Function and Procedures

The yearly meeting will receive written reports from its committees and from its constituent meetings, signed by the proper officers. It will review the state of our yearly meeting and consider communications addressed to it. It will hear and act upon the concerns of its members pertaining to the work and influence of the Society of Friends in general.

It should exercise a general oversight and care of subordinate meetings in things pertaining to the welfare of our Society in general.

The yearly meeting provides for the due consideration of epistles and traveling minutes of Friends from other Friends yearly meetings.

All letters and papers addressed to the yearly meeting, regarding which the clerk desires counsel, may be referred to the Executive Committee, which should consider them, and advise whether to have them presented for the consideration of the yearly meeting.

The yearly meeting needs information concerning its constituent meetings, so that it can aid committees in their work, give a knowledge of conditions, and extend sympathetic help to the smaller meetings which need encouragement and assistance from the larger body.

The many practical details of how the yearly meeting fulfills its responsibilities through its officers, committees, and staff are collected in the OVYM Handbook. This is updated on a regular basis to accurately reflect current practice.

EXECUTIVE COMMITTEE

Duties

The Executive Committee transacts business for the yearly meeting between its annual sessions in all cases where the welfare of our Society makes this desirable, and carries out instructions given it by the yearly meeting.

Meeting Structure, Function and Procedures

In general its duties should include printing and distributing Friendly literature, furnishing forms to monthly meetings for use in keeping records of members, transfers, births, marriages, and deaths, maintaining a current list of members with their addresses, endeavoring to extend the knowledge of our principles, rendering advice and assistance to meetings in the matter of property and trusts, and to individuals who feel the need of support in maintaining our testimonies. The committee shall keep in close and sympathetic touch with other committees appointed by the yearly meeting in all cases when that body is not in session, but it shall not make changes in this *Book of Faith and Practice* or issue any statement of faith.

Meetings

The committee may fix its own times of meeting, except that its clerk shall call special meetings upon the request of three members of the committee. The clerk of each monthly meeting as well as appointed representatives should be notified of each committee meeting. It is advised that important action be taken only after the judgment of the committee has been obtained.

Minutes

The committee shall keep full and complete minutes; rendering to the yearly meeting reports of all business transacted.

Method of Appointment

Each monthly meeting shall appoint one or more members to represent it on the Executive Committee. The clerk and treasurer of the yearly meeting shall also be members of the Executive Committee by reason of their appointments. The yearly meeting, if it wishes to do so, may appoint members at large in addition to those named by the monthly meetings.

Meeting Structure, Function and Procedures

NOMINATING COMMITTEE

The Executive Committee shall determine the method of populating the nominating committee of the yearly meeting, which then nominates all officers, including the clerks and members of committees of the yearly meeting. The Nominating Committee shall meet for this purpose soon after appointment, at least one month before the annual sessions of the yearly meeting begin, and at other times as necessary.

Nominating Committee is responsible for offering names to the yearly meeting for appointment as representatives to Friends General Conference, Friends World Committee for Consultation, American Friends Service Committee, Friends Committee on National Legislation, and other organizations as the need arises.

ANNUAL STATISTICAL REPORT

Annual statistical reports shall be made by the monthly meetings to the yearly meeting, containing all needed information on a form provided by the yearly meeting for the purpose. The information asked for should include data on changes in membership status (births, deaths, admissions, removals, etc.), attendance in First Day Schools, attenders at Quaker schools, changes in times and places of meetings for worship, and other necessary information. The yearly meeting may from time to time ask for additional information not included on the form.

Queries

The queries invite Friends, both individually and as a meeting, to examine themselves periodically relative to the grounding principles that Friends have established. Faithful consideration of the queries in openness to the Spirit has been found to enrich the life of the meeting and its members.

Meeting Structure, Function and Procedures

Friends have found different ways to make use of the queries. Some read them as a starting point for personal inward reflection. Meetings may consider a query in a period of meditation and worship at the beginning of their business meetings. It is good practice to consider each query at least once a year. A meeting's responses to the queries may provide a basis for writing its annual state of the meeting report. The presentation of the queries to the local meeting is the responsibility of the clerk unless assigned to a committee, such as the Committee for Ministry and Counsel.

First Query
What is Quakerism or the Quaker way? What does that mean to me?
What marks our meeting as Quaker?

Second Query
What does worship mean to me, and how do I worship?
How does our meeting worship as a community?

Third Query
What helps me seek divine guidance in business meeting?
How does our meeting seek and follow the group's spiritual discernment in our meetings for business?

Fourth Query
What spiritual disciplines enliven my spirit?
How does our meeting facilitate spiritual growth?

Fifth Query
What binds me to my meeting community?
What fosters mutual love and communion in our meeting? How does our meeting resolve conflicts when they arise?

Sixth Query
How do I seek to act with integrity? How do I follow the ever-opening pathway of Truth?
How does my meeting help me to be faithful?

Seventh Query
How does simplicity guide my days?
How does our meeting practice simplicity?

Meeting Structure, Function and Procedures

Eighth Query

How is my life a daily example of nonviolence?
How does our meeting nurture peace in the wider community?

Ninth Query

How do I live in harmony with all creation?
How does our meeting community exercise responsible stewardship?

Tenth Query

How do I affirm that of God in everyone?
In what ways is our meeting an open and affirming community, welcoming to all? In what ways do we need to grow?

Eleventh Query

How have I fallen short in the past year?
When has our meeting avoided doing things that are hard to do?

Twelfth Query

Where have I experienced the Divine Mystery in my life?
How do we keep the Divine Spirit at the center of the life of our meeting?

Faith & Practice Revision

Proposals to change this *Book of Faith and Practice* may originate in the monthly meeting, and if so, they should receive the approval of the quarterly meeting, and then be transmitted to the yearly meeting for final action; or they may originate in the annual sessions of the yearly meeting itself. In this case, final action may not be taken until the following year after the proposed change has appeared in the minutes of the yearly meeting or has been presented in a printed form for approval.

OTHER QUAKER ORGANIZATIONS

Over the course of the last hundred years, dozens of Quaker organizations have grown up to provide service to Friends and to promote Quaker values in the wider world. Ohio Valley Yearly Meeting has made financial contributions to many, and members of Ohio Valley Yearly Meeting meetings were involved in many more. A few of the larger and more influential organizations are listed below. Further information about Quaker organizations can be found on their websites.

Friends General Conference

In 2015 there were 36 yearly meetings and associations in the United States and Canada. These are classified in five groups: Friends General Conference (FGC), Friends United Meeting, Evangelical Friends-International, Conservative Friends, and several independent yearly meetings. In addition, there is a small but significant number of monthly meetings with no yearly meeting affiliation. Ohio Valley Yearly Meeting belongs to FGC.

FGC emerged from several gatherings among Hicksite Quakers. These started in 1868 with the Biennial First Day School Conference. The Friends Union for Philanthropic Labor began meeting at the same time and in the same location in 1882; the Friends Educational Conference scheduled joint meetings starting in 1896. They formally joined together as the Friends General Conference in 1900 as a way of bringing Friends in the United States and Canada together across yearly meeting lines to share their experiences, exchange ideas, and develop programs that nurture and stimulate the religious life of the Society of Friends in individual monthly meetings as well as the larger community of Friends.

Other Quaker Organizations

Seven Hicksite yearly meetings were initially involved: Indiana (now known as Ohio Valley), Baltimore, Genesee, Illinois, New York, Ohio, and Philadelphia. In 2015, FGC had grown to an association of 14 yearly meetings, supplemented with regional groups and a number of directly affiliated monthly meetings. Its stated purpose is, with divine guidance, to nurture the spiritual vitality of the Religious Society of Friends by providing programs and services for Friends, meetings, and seekers.

The character and thrust of FGC has been largely determined by the conviction that the same Spirit that was revealed in the Scriptures can lead men and women today, that Quaker worship should be based on expectant waiting for divine guidance, and that there is an enriching potential in theological diversity.

Being an association of meetings, FGC has no authority over its constituent meetings, which fully retain their autonomy. Policy and the program planning of the Conference are determined by a Central Committee appointed by the member yearly meetings. Its annual Gatherings are not business meetings, but conferences to which all Friends are invited.

American Friends Service Committee

Refusal to participate in war has been an enduring Quaker concern ever since George Fox said in 1651 that he "lived in the virtue of that life and power that took away the occasion of all wars."[29] Friends have maintained with consistency, and often with much suffering, the belief that the power of love and the spirit of justice are the only bases for resolving international disputes.

World War I sharply questioned the validity of this testimony. Friends found themselves faced with the necessity for profound reconsideration and for active work in support of this great principle. Their most cogent argument was fearless and impartial service to the

Other Quaker Organizations

victims of war. During the struggle, the vision and leadership of Rufus Jones brought together all branches and all types of Friends in the effort to convey help and a message of love to the people of Europe. The founding of the American Friends Service Committee (AFSC) ensued on April 30, 1917 by Friends representing several areas of Quakerism. They were deeply concerned for the spiritual values endangered by America's entrance into the war, and to provide constructive, non-military service to young men who were conscientious objectors.

The work of the AFSC has evolved over the last century in response to changing conditions and to reflect the concerns and testimonies of Friends in the United States.

Friends World Committee for Consultation

Friends World Committee for Consultation (FWCC) was established by a minute of a World Conference of the Religious Society of Friends held at Swarthmore, Pennsylvania in 1937. The purpose of the Friends World Committee for Consultation is to encourage fellowship among all the branches of the Religious Society of Friends. To advance this goal, it publishes material of interest to all Friends, encourages intervisitation, holds conferences and promotes Quaker concerns.

Yearly meetings and similar organized groups of Friends throughout the world who are affiliated with FWCC send representatives to its World Plenary Meetings. A representative Interim Committee is appointed at each meeting to assist staff and officers of the organization's world headquarters, located in London. In addition, Friends World Committee for Consultation has formed geographic sections, which have their own officers and staff to carry on regional concerns: Africa Section; Asia and West Pacific Section; European and Middle East Section; and Section of the Americas.

Other Quaker Organizations

Quaker United Nations Office

FWCC sponsored the Quaker United Nations Office (QUNO) in 1947. A unique role is played both in New York and Geneva by the Quaker House close to the offices of the United Nations, where delegates from opposing factions can meet informally and search for ways to reconcile their differences. QUNO staff also provide information to Friends about the U.N. and arrange for Friends and others to attend seminars and U.N. sessions so that they may better understand the work of this world organization.

Friends Committee on National Legislation

Founded in 1943 by a group of Friends gathered at Quaker Hill in Richmond, Indiana, the Friends Committee on National Legislation (FCNL) is the oldest religious lobby in Washington D.C. While the FNCL does not speak for all Friends in the United States, its policymaking body consists of appointees from worshipping bodies of Friends throughout the United States. It has long been and continues to be effective in presenting the viewpoints of Friends to members of Congress and to the executive branch of government.

Friends Journal

Quakers have been publishing fliers, pamphlets, and tracts since the 1650s. Periodicals became particularly important to the North American Friends in the 19th century as Quakers settled across the continent and visitation by traveling ministers became more difficult. With the separations of the 1820s and later, Friends in different branches produced publications to serve their own members. Two of these were published by Friends in the two Philadelphia Yearly Meetings: *The Friends Intelligencer* (Hicksite) and *The Friend* (Orthodox). After these meetings reunited in 1955, *Friends Journal*

Other Quaker Organizations

was created as an independent organization, "for the purpose of promoting religious concerns of the Religious Society of Friends and the education and information of its members and others by means of the written or spoken word." In 2015, the *Journal* had readers in all 50 states and in more than 40 other countries.

Friends Journal also sponsors *QuakerSpeak*, a Quaker YouTube channel that presents personal and intimate interviews. It seeks to give viewers worldwide an experience that is entertaining, informative, inspiring, challenging, inviting, unifying and collaborative.

Quaker Earthcare Witness

Originally named Friends Committee on Unity with Nature, this organization was established in 1987. A workshop was held at the FGC Gathering that year on the importance of living in harmony with the earth and with all of God's creation. Its name was officially changed to Quaker Earthcare Witness (QEW) in 2003. Although it started at an FGC gathering, the organization works with all Quaker branches.

QEW's purpose is to call on all people to live in right relationship with all creation, recognizing that the entire world is interconnected, and is a manifestation of God. The organization works to integrate into the beliefs and practices of the Religious Society of Friends the truth that God's creation is to be respected, protected, and held in reverence in its own right; and the truth that human aspirations for peace and justice depend upon restoring the earth's ecological integrity. It promotes these truths by being patterns and examples, by communicating its message, and by providing spiritual and material support to those engaged in the compelling task of transforming our relationship to the earth.

A BRIEF HISTORY

The Beginnings of Quakerism

The Religious Society of Friends originated in England at the time of the Puritan Revolution (about 1642-1660). There was a growing sense of personal religious independence among the people that resulted in the temporary overthrow of the monarchy and the installation of Oliver Cromwell as Lord Protector. Dissatisfaction with the established church resulted in many quick-growing, but often short-lived, sects and in a large number of restless, searching spirits.

George Fox (1624-1691), one of the first Quakers, was of this seeking type of mind. Born in 1624, he began when nineteen years old a solitary, spiritual quest for Truth. He recorded in his *Journal* that at last in 1646, "when all my hopes in...all men were gone, so that I had nothing outwardly to help me, nor could tell what to do, then, Oh then, I heard a voice which said, 'There is one, even Christ Jesus, that can speak to thy condition,' and, when I heard it, my heart did leap for joy."[30]

In 1647 Fox began to preach, convincing many people, and in 1648 a whole community in Nottinghamshire accepted his message and, associating together, called themselves Children of the Light, the earliest name by which Friends were known. From this time on, the number of his followers grew rapidly.

Puritan ministers then taught that God's revelation to humanity lay only in the work of the historic Christ as recorded in the Bible and that, until the judgment at the Second Coming, God would not speak again. Fox proclaimed that God speaks directly to each human soul through an immediate, living experience of revelation, the Inward Light of Christ, requiring no human mediator to translate God's meaning to the individual.

A Brief History

George Fox was a powerful personality. In *The Beginnings of Quakerism*, William Braithwaite described him as having "combined in a singular degree the burning zeal of the enthusiast with the magnetic force of a born leader of men" and such was the power of the truth he and other early Friends preached, "that a single man or woman living in the spirit of the apostles and prophets would shake all the country...for ten miles round."[31]

He soon attracted a group of young men and women who became inspired preachers of this new religious force; they were called Publishers of Truth. These were joined by other earnest men and women. They engaged in the difficult work of spreading the movement, traveling in twos and threes throughout the length and breadth of England and extending their labors into Wales, Scotland, and Ireland, although often hindered by imprisonment and persecution. Undismayed by every sort of difficulty, they fed the inward spiritual flame of widely separated groups, stimulating their zeal, holding them in the bond of group-consciousness, and providing for them a channel of communication.

Margaret Fell (1614-1702), often called the Mother of Quakerism, was an early convert and an equally powerful personality. Swarthmoor Hall, her home, became a center of activity, a stable focal point giving the movement a sense of community and strength. She set up a central fund to help those on long preaching trips, in prison, in isolated meetings, and later to promote the establishment of women's meetings. Eleven years after the death of her husband, Judge Thomas Fell, she and George Fox were married.

The powerful preaching of these leaders was supported by the daily life of the first Friends. Along with an intense religious fervor there ran a life of practical righteousness. Justice, temperance, commercial honesty, and observance of all civil laws that did not violate their conscience were vitally important matters. Braithwaite wrote, "None could dispute the validity of a Christianity which resulted in consistent and Christ-touched lives. In such lives, amid

A Brief History

all their imperfections, the Inward Light was justified of its children."[32]

A deep realization of the equality of all persons before God led to the early recognition of the spiritual gifts of women as equal to those of men and the acceptance of their public preaching. Among other outward behaviors, it also brought about the use of the "plain" language and Friends' refusal to remove their hats in the presence of those deemed their social superiors—customs which caused frequent persecution. Still greater suffering resulted from their refusal to take oaths or to pay tithes for the upkeep of the state church.

With the restoration of the monarchy in 1660, the Anglican Church was re-established as the official religion of the state and no other worship was permitted. An era of persecution was inaugurated for all religious non-conformists. Most religious dissenters went into hiding, but Friends persisted and endured long imprisonments, disastrous fines, and cruel treatment. Their meetings were often broken up and meetinghouses destroyed. But because their consciences assured them that resistance to an unjust law was no sin, they maintained their way of worship openly and bravely despite every effort to stop them. In some places, when all adult Friends were jailed, the children continued to hold meetings for worship alone.

Faithfulness in persisting according to their religious convictions, with no evasion of the penalties of the law, was an important factor in finally winning legal recognition for liberty of conscience and religious toleration. But for the Society of Friends itself, the persecution had some unfortunate results: it restricted the itinerant services of the Publishers of Truth, isolated meetings, and hastened the necessity for organizing what had been a glorious creative movement into a sect.

From 1667 on, George Fox was active in helping to organize the system of monthly, quarterly, and yearly meetings and in arranging

A Brief History

their methods of procedure. Women's business meetings were set up in addition to men's. A Meeting of Ministers and a Meeting for Sufferings (at first, this was a body concerned with assisting those suffering persecution and their families; it developed into a yearly meeting Executive Committee) were established.

The earliest concerns of these business meetings were to provide for the poor and prisoners, to check the vagaries of individual judgment, to admonish delinquents, to provide for carrying on work at home, to cover the expenses of ministers traveling beyond the seas, and to keep accurate records. While the discipline thus set up was no equivalent for the compelling power of widespread evangelism, it did foster well-ordered and noble lives.

Efforts at formulation of doctrine soon followed, and in this, Robert Barclay (1648-1690) and William Penn (1644-1718) were the foremost figures. Barclay's most complete exposition was his *Apology*. His Quakerism was affected by current Puritan theology. The influence of their writings was so great as to be felt as late as the nineteenth century when various separations occurred within the Religious Society of Friends.

The development of the early movement into a sect was underway. Along with the formulation of doctrine there were growing experiments toward improving the social order. These included justice toward workmen and employees, and efforts to reestablish the poor in business, along with plans for giving work to those in prison, the establishment of humane workhouses, and active concern for the treatment of the insane. Temperance and the question of slavery claimed the attention of Friends. In the colonies of Pennsylvania and Rhode Island bold attempts were made to establish truly Christian commonwealths.

A Brief History

Friends in the American Colonies

As early as 1655 the New World had attracted Friends. Efforts were made during the following years to plant the seeds of Quakerism in Massachusetts, New York, and Virginia. In the latter two colonies there was some persecution, but the martyrs of Quakerism in America met their test in Massachusetts. Everything that the authorities could devise was tried to stop the spread of Quaker Truth in this colony. Harrowing tortures were endured, many underwent punishment again and again, and four suffered death. After ten years of persecution, they succeeded in breaking down the intolerant laws.

During this period, an early haven was found in Rhode Island, where the first meeting in the New World was established. This colony became the center of New England Quakerism. Its long line of Quaker Governors and men in public positions did eminent service in the political life of the colony until the time of the Revolutionary War.

A period of expansion followed George Fox's visit to America in 1671-1673. New meetings were established in New York, Maryland, Virginia, and the Carolinas, and in greater numbers in New Jersey and, a decade later, in Pennsylvania.

These last two colonies had been opened for settlement later than the others, but conditions were especially favorable. West Jersey was bought by a group of Friends in 1674 and in 1681 Pennsylvania was granted to William Penn, so that there Quakers had freedom and peace and unparalleled opportunity to try out their ability to conduct a Christian government. William Penn was a statesman of high order, an outstanding advocate of justice for Native Americans, and a champion of liberty of conscience. He designed a government based on advanced ideas of civil and religious liberty and equality, which was a forerunner of that laid out in the Constitution of the United States. Friends maintained almost absolute political control of Pennsylvania until 1740 and were a power for fifteen years longer, when measures by the colonial government to support military action in the French and Indian War led most to resign from the Assembly. At this time, Friends largely withdrew from all participation in government and political life.

Penn's initially successful policy of Friends toward Native Americans was the outcome of their sense of justice and their conviction that before God all persons are equal, irrespective of their color. These principles also came to be expressed in their attitudes on another great question—that of slavery. In 1671 George Fox had advised giving slaves their freedom after a period of years. Philadelphia Yearly Meeting advised against the slave trade in 1696, and such sentiment grew slowly until 1758 when John Woolman made a moving plea for the liberty of slaves and began the great work of his life. He aroused Friends in both America and England, many of whom became influential actors and tireless workers until slavery was finally abolished.

Friends' opposition to war largely took them out of public life. This fact together with the increasing influence within the Society of Quietism caused a profound transformation in the Society. More and more Friends in the latter half of the 18th century withdrew as much as possible from involvement with the outside world and centered upon perfecting their own spiritual lives. They built a "hedge" around their Society with the rules and customs of a peculiar people. This preserved some valuable features, but it also brought a narrowing introspection that was fertile ground for controversy.

The Second Period of Quakerism

Early in the 19th century two very divergent tendencies could be seen within Quakerism. One was toward a zealous evangelicalism which was fostered by a number of prominent Quaker ministers, some of whom came over from England, and was accelerated by the

A Brief History

popular rise of the Methodist movement. The other was toward a reaffirmation of the centrality of the Inward Light of Christ as a sufficient basis for faith. Job Scott, a saintly man and true mystic, and Elias Hicks, a prophetic minister, were the chief spokesmen for the latter.

The chasm grew steadily wider until 1827 when a separation occurred in Philadelphia Yearly Meeting. This tragedy was due to lack of historical knowledge, lack of spiritual understanding and lack of love for one another, and was followed by withdrawals by one side or the other in many other meetings, forming so-called "Hicksite" and so-called "Orthodox" branches. Further separations occurred over the last 200 years, resulting in the fractured Society seen today.

Yet the 19th century did contain some advances in Quaker development. A great migration of Friends into new territory in the Midwest took place and new yearly meetings in Ohio, Indiana, Iowa, and Illinois were established.

The retirement of Friends from public affairs also helped to stimulate their zeal for purely moral causes, such as the abolition of slavery, concern for the welfare of African-Americans and Native Americans, the work for social morality, the suppression of liquor traffic, and prison reform.

The women's rights movement grew out of the involvement of Quaker women in the anti-slavery movement. By publicly and extensively lecturing against slavery, they did much to break down the barrier against women speaking in public. Lucretia Mott, a Quaker minister and abolitionist, along with Mary Ann M'Clintock, Martha Coffin Wright, Jane Hunt, and Elizabeth Cady Stanton, organized the Seneca Falls Convention in 1848, which marked the formal beginning of the organized crusade for the rights of women.

A Brief History

Education has been a deep concern of Friends from their earliest history, and monthly meeting schools, boarding schools, and colleges have been established.

History of Ohio Valley Yearly Meeting

During the early 18th Century many Friends were attracted southward into Virginia and the Carolinas and some became involved in the institution of slavery. As a result of the labors of Francis Daniel Pastorius, William Southeby, Benjamin Lay, John Woolman, Anthony Benezet, Sarah Grimké, Angelina Grimké Weld, Lucretia Mott, Levi and Catherine Coffin, Sophia Sturge and others, Friends came to believe slavery a curse; and slowly the conscience of the Society of Friends was awakened to the evil. Following the Revolutionary War, many Friends in the South decided to migrate to the slave-free lands in the Northwest Territory to begin a new life.

The migration to the Waynesville, Ohio area began in 1799 when Abijah O'Neal and his family left Bush River, South Carolina, and settled on some 3,000 acres on the east bank of the Little Miami River north of Caesar's Creek. Within 15 years, more than 18,000 Quakers from the Carolinas and Georgia had left the land of slavery and made for the North to find a new home. Others came to the Miami country from Pennsylvania, New Jersey, and other seaboard states.

In April 1801, twelve families (81 individuals) in the Waynesville area began meeting for worship in a member's home. Near the end of that year they sent a request to Westland Meeting, Pennsylvania (Baltimore Yearly Meeting) to hold meetings for worship on Sundays and Thursdays. This request was granted in September 1802. Early in 1803 they asked Redstone Quarterly Meeting for permission to establish a monthly meeting; and when the request was approved, Miami Monthly Meeting was opened on October 13, 1803. Its eastern boundary was the Hocking River, the southern was the Ohio

A Brief History

River, but there was no limit to the north or to the west. During this period of migration, hundreds of Friends from the Carolinas and Georgia brought their membership to Miami Monthly Meeting, until such time as other meetings could be established in the Northwest Territory. By 1815, Miami Monthly Meeting was said to have the largest membership of any Friends Meeting in Quakerdom.

After its establishment in 1803, Miami Monthly Meeting set off many new Meetings. Among the earliest ones were Lees Creek, Hardin Creek, Caesar's Creek, West Branch, Elk, Center and Whitewater. In 1807 Miami, West Branch and Center Monthly Meetings requested that a new quarterly meeting be established to be known as Miami Quarterly Meeting and held at Waynesville, Ohio, on the second Saturday in February, May, August and November. Baltimore Yearly Meeting having approved the request, Miami Quarterly Meeting was opened in May 1809. The building of the White Brick Meetinghouse at Waynesville was begun in 1811 to accommodate the Quarterly Meeting.

In 1812, Baltimore Yearly Meeting granted permission to the quarterly meetings west of the Allegheny Mountains to form Ohio Yearly Meeting. The first session was held at Short Creek on the 14th of August 1813. The Ohio Yearly Meeting included all meetings in Ohio, Indiana Territory and adjacent areas of Pennsylvania and Virginia.

In 1820, Miami Quarterly Meeting proposed that all Meetings in Illinois, Indiana, and western Ohio be formed into a new yearly meeting. The quarterly meetings making up the proposed yearly meeting were Miami, West Branch, Fairfield, Whitewater, and Blue River Quarterlies. Ohio Yearly Meeting approved the proposal, and the first session of Indiana Yearly Meeting was held in the Whitewater (Richmond, Indiana) Meetinghouse on August 10, 1821.

When separation occurred in 1828, the Yearly Meeting split into two bodies: Indiana Yearly Meeting (Orthodox), and Indiana Yearly Meeting (Hicksite). At Waynesville, the Hicksite body retained the

A Brief History

meetinghouse. However, in many other cases west of the Alleghenies, the Orthodox body retained it.

For nearly 150 years, there were two bodies known as Indiana Yearly Meeting. In 1975, it seemed desirable for Indiana Yearly Meeting of Friends General Conference to change its name to eliminate the avoidable confusion resulting from identical official names and to better identify the area included in its membership. For these reasons, in 1976, the name was changed to Ohio Valley Yearly Meeting.

The Yearly Meeting is composed of two Quarters: Miami and Whitewater.

In 2020, Whitewater Quarter consists of Bloomington, Clear Creek (Richmond), Fall Creek (Pendleton), Fort Wayne, Lafayette, North Meadow Circle (Indianapolis), and White Rose (Wabash) Monthly Meetings in Indiana.

Miami Quarter consists of Campus (Wilmington), Community (Cincinnati), Dayton, Eastern Hills (Cincinnati), Miami (Waynesville), Oxford, and Yellow Springs Monthly Meetings in Ohio, as well as Lexington and Louisville Monthly Meetings in Kentucky.

GLOSSARY

Advices: Friends have found it useful to regularly remind one another of shared qualities. Advices touch on the foundations of true, personal discipline, on the care of our children, on family life, and on the character of our day-to-day living.

Answer that of God: To recognize and respond to the presence of the divine within others.

Affirmation: A legal declaration made by Friends or others who conscientiously decline to take an oath.

Assistant Clerk: A person who assists a clerk and is prepared to fill in when the clerk is unable to act.

Associate Member: A minor child recorded as a member at the request of parents, one or both of whom are members of the monthly meeting.

Birthright Member: Historically, a Friend born of at least one Quaker parent and recorded at birth on the membership rolls of the meeting (Note: this status is no longer used in Ohio Valley Yearly Meeting.).

Breaking Meeting: The act of closing of the meeting for worship when a designated person or persons shake hands with those seated next to them.

Business Meeting: see **Meeting for Business** below.

Center Down: To endeavor to still our conscious thoughts, clear our minds, and open ourselves to hear God speak directly to us.

Clear: A sense of having said and done all that the Lord has asked of you.

Clearness: Confidence that a proposed action is consistent with the divine will.

Glossary

Clearness Committee:

(1) Friends appointed to help determine the clearness of persons intending marriage with each other, and of the meeting to take their marriage under its care.

(2) A committee appointed to assist a person who is considering membership in the meeting.

(3) A committee to assist one or more persons to discern the right way forward with respect to a decision or concern.

Clerk: see **Presiding Clerk** below.

Committee for Ministry and Counsel: A monthly meeting committee appointed to focus on the meeting for worship and the spiritual well-being of the meeting community. (See **Fostering the Meeting for Worship** on page 46 and **Pastoral Care** on page 47.)

Communion: To be drawn as a community into direct spiritual communication with God and with each other.

Concern: A quickening sense of the need to do something about a situation or issue in response to what is felt to be a direct intimation of God's will. A concern, whether of an individual or a monthly meeting, implies an interest so deep and vigorous that it often moves to action.

Consensus: A term used in the secular world to indicate unanimous agreement. Among Friends, it is sometimes used loosely as a synonym for **Sense of the Meeting** (below).

Continuing Revelation: The belief that God still speaks to people directly and, in so doing, may reveal God's desires or directions directly to an individual or to a group of people.

Convinced Friend: A member who has been led to become a Friend by the Inner Teacher after contemplation, prayer, and inward seeking.

Glossary

Corporate Discernment: A group's best understanding of where God is leading them.

Corporate Leading: Divine guidance for a group of Friends.

Correspondent: The person responsible for the transmission, reception, and acknowledgement of communications sent from or to a meeting, frequently the presiding clerk.

Discernment: Spiritual understanding or insight and the ability to apply these to spiritual matters; the wisdom to distinguish Truth from other impressions.

Elder: An individual who fosters ministry in meeting for worship, the spiritual life of the meeting, and of the individuals in it.

Eldering: Lovingly expressing concern, tenderly questioning an individual's behavior, and encouraging improvement.

Epistle: A public letter of greeting and ministry; sent from a Friends meeting or organization to other Friends groups to supply information, spiritual insight, and encouragement.

First Day School: Sunday religious education programs provided for children and adults (called Sunday School by other religious bodies).

Gathered Meeting: Those special occasions when a meeting for worship attains a greater than usual sense of the Divine Presence, touching the hearts of all, and uniting them in a common experience of holy fellowship.

Good Order: Procedures for the conduct of business and witness that encourage a meeting to carry out its corporate activities under divine leading.

Gospel Order: A term used by George Fox and others to describe the covenant order of the church. It concerns how we live in faithful relationship with God, each other, and all of creation.

Glossary

Handbook: The many practical details of how the yearly meeting fulfills its responsibilities through its officers, committees, and staff are collected in the OVYM Handbook. This is updated on a regular basis to accurately reflect current practice.

Hold in the Light:

(1) To desire that divine guidance and healing will be present for an individual who is in distress or faces a difficult situation.

(2) To give prayerful consideration to an idea.

In the face of: In the presence of. Often used to refer to the approval of minutes during the business meeting or committee meeting in which they were taken.

Inner Light: see **Inward Light** below.

Inward Light: The direct, unmediated experience of the Divine; often just "the Light." Other terms found in Quaker writings are: the Spirit, the Spirit of Truth, the Divine Principle, the Seed, the Guide, the Christ Within, the Inward Teacher, and that of God in every person.

Leading:

(1) A sense of being called by God to undertake a specific course of action, often arising in response to a concern.

(2) Direct guidance from the Holy Spirit in right ways of living.

Letter of Introduction: A brief letter to Friends in other meetings, stating that the person named in it is a member in good standing.

Light of Christ: see **Inward Light** above.

Light Within: see **Inward Light** above.

Meeting for Business: A business meeting conducted under the immediate guidance of the Holy Spirit.

Glossary

Meeting for Sufferings:

(1) Originally, a committee to support and care for members (and their families) who suffered imprisonment or other hardship because of their commitment to Friends principles.

(2) In some yearly meetings, the official name of the yearly meeting's executive committee.

Meeting for Worship: In Ohio Valley Yearly Meeting, held with minimal pre-planning. Friends gather at a specified time and place in silence, waiting on the leadings of the Spirit. Some Friends may offer vocal ministry to the meeting or it may be entirely silent.

Meetinghouse: The building a Friends Meeting gathers in.

Mind the Light: An expression used to remind Friends that the Inward Light can reveal God's will and directions to us. Minding the Light calls for both active obedience to divine leadings and carefully nurturing openness to the Light.

Ministers: Members who are recognized by a monthly meeting as having a special gift, either in speaking or in other forms of service.

Ministry: Sharing or acting upon one's gifts, whether speaking during a meeting for worship or in service to individuals, to the meeting, or to the larger community.

Minute: The record of corporate unity reached during a business meeting.

Monthly Meeting:

(1) The fundamental working unit of the Society of Friends.

(2) A body of Friends who meet regularly for worship and to conduct business.

(3) The monthly business meeting (see **Meeting for Business** above).

Glossary

Moved of the Spirit: Led or prompted by God.

Moved to Speak: A clear sense of being urged by the Divine Spirit to offer vocal ministry.

Notions: Beliefs which are out of harmony with Truths of God.

Opening: A spiritual insight or leading.

Opportunity: A spontaneous period of worship, especially one that occurs when a traveling minister visits Friends in their homes.

Out of Unity: Not in harmony with Friends principles and testimonies.

Overseers: Members of an Oversight Committee (Note: Because of its historic relationship with slavery, this term is no longer in general use).

Oversight: Pastoral care and nurture of members and attenders.

Oversight Committee:

(1) Historically, the committee that provided pastoral care.

(2) In some contemporary meetings, the committee that facilitates a wedding.

Plain Speech: The practice of early Friends to use "thee, thy, thou, and thine" when addressing a single person; and to refer to the days of the week and months of the year with numbers (e.g., First Day for Sunday and Third Month for March).

Preparative Meeting: A group under the care of an established monthly meeting which gathers for worship at another place. (Note: The origin of the term dates from the time when most monthly meetings were composed of multiple preparative meetings that "prepared business" for their joint monthly business meeting.)

Glossary

Presiding Clerk: The person who conducts business meetings and committee meetings, often assisted by an assistant clerk and a recording clerk.

Proceed as Way Opens: To wait for divine guidance when seeking to solve a problem or address a concern. This may result from a time of active seeking or arrive unexpectedly. Frequently, it points to a previously unforeseen way forward.

Programmed Meeting: In many other yearly meetings, a meeting for worship conducted by a designated leader with a predetermined program, often including music, scripture reading, an offering, sermon, etc. Most programmed meetings among Friends include a period of waiting worship.

Quaker: A member of the Religious Society of Friends.

Quarterly Meeting:

(1) A collection of monthly meetings within a yearly meeting.

(2) The gatherings of members of a quarterly meeting, traditionally on four occasions each year, now usually three times per year.

Queries: Questions based on Quaker practices and testimonies which are used by meetings and individuals to examine their individual and corporate lives and to guide their actions.

Recorded Minister: A member who is recognized by a monthly meeting as having the gift of vocal ministry or a special gift of service to the meeting or the wider community.

Recorder: see **Statistician** below.

Recording Clerk: The person appointed to record minutes at business meetings.

Released Friend: A member who has been released from the normal obligations of membership in order to fulfill a leading as approved by the meeting.

Rightly Ordered: see **Good Order** above.

Glossary

Seekers: People who are actively in search of the transcendent.

Sense of the Meeting: A decision on an issue or concern which is considered to be in accordance with the divine will. This is usually discerned by the presiding clerk and formulated into a proposed minute (see **Corporate Discernment**).

Silent Worship: see **Meeting for Worship** above.

Sojourning Member: A member who is temporarily residing at a distance from the Friend's home meeting and whose home meeting has approved acting as a member of another, closer meeting.

Speak to One's Condition: To experience another person's words or actions as uniquely inspired to settle one's spiritual condition, help solve a problem, or point to a right decision.

Stand Aside: An action taken during a meeting for business by an individual who has genuine reservations about a particular decision, but also recognizes that the decision is supported by the weight of the meeting.

Stand in the Way: An action taken by a member in a meeting for business who feels unable to join in a decision (see **Stop** or **Stop in the Mind** below) on which there is otherwise unity. This is a privilege granted by the community, not an inherent right of any individual to block an action.

Statistician: The person responsible for maintaining a meeting's membership records, including births, marriages, removals, and deaths among members, and for recording the attendance at meetings for worship.

Stewardship: Caring for money, property, and other resources as if they belonged to God.

Stop or **Stop in the Mind:** A clear sense of spiritual uneasiness in the face of a proposed decision or action that makes one unable to follow it.

Glossary

Take under the Care: The decision by a meeting to accept responsibility for and to give oversight to an activity, program, or event. Among other things, this includes a marriage, the ministry of an individual, or a worship group.

Testimony: The visible manifestation of our relationships with God. This is an outward action flowing naturally from our experience of God's call.

Threshing Session: A form of business meeting in which only a single (usually controversial) issue is considered in a way that is free from the necessity of reaching a decision.

Traveling Minute: A statement of endorsement that a monthly meeting gives to a member who feels called to visit other meetings and Friends groups to share a concern.

Treasurer: An individual designated by the meeting to manage its financial resources.

Truth: Traditionally, Friends capitalized this word to refer to the revealed will of God as best discerned by a meeting under the guidance of the Inward Light.

Unity: The sense of spiritual oneness and harmony whose realization is a primary objective of a meeting for worship or a meeting for business (see **Sense of the Meeting** above).

Unprogrammed Meeting: see **Meeting for Worship** above.

Vocal Ministry: To speak, sing, or pray aloud during a meeting for worship.

Waiting Worship: see **Meeting for Worship** above.

Way Opens:

(1) To have an inward, spiritual block removed.

(2) To receive divine guidance when seeking to solve a seemingly intractable problem or address a concern.

Glossary

Weighty Member: An informal term for a Friend who is respected for spiritual depth, wisdom, and long service to the Religious Society of Friends.

Worship Group: A group of people who meet for worship, but do not conduct business. This may be formed under the care of a monthly meeting or by the gathering together of people outside of the yearly meeting structure.

Worship Sharing: A group practice that acknowledges the presence of God during which participants share personal experiences and feelings in response to a prearranged theme or a set of questions.

Yearly Meeting:

(1) A designated set of monthly meetings from a geographically extended area.

(2) The annual business meetings of Friends from a designated group of monthly meetings.

SUGGESTED READING LIST

Margery Abbott, *To Be Broken and Tender: A Quaker Theology for Today*, Western Friend / Friends Bulletin Corporation, 2010

Rex Ambler, *The Quaker Way: A Rediscovery*, Winchester, United Kingdom & Washington: Christian Alternative Books, 2013

Robert Barclay, *Barclay's Apology in Modern English*, Dean Freiday (ed), Newberg, OR: The Barclay Press, 1991

Michael Birkel, *Silence and Witness*, Maryknoll, New York: Orbis Books, 2004

Paul Buckley, *Primitive Quakerism Revived: Living as Friends in the Twenty-First Century*, San Francisco: Inner Light Books, 2018

Sandra Cronk, *Gospel Order: A Quaker Understanding of Faithful Quaker Community*, Wallingford, Pennsylvania: Pendle Hill Pamphlet 297, 1991

George Fox, *The Journal of George Fox*, John L. Nickalls (ed), London: Religious Society of Friends, 1975

George Fox, *The Power of the Lord is Over All: The Pastoral Letters of George Fox*, T. Canby Jones (ed), Richmond, IN: Friends United Press, 1989

Mary Garman, Judith Applegate, Margaret Benefiel, and Dortha Meredith (eds), *Hidden in Plain Sight: Quaker Women's Writings, 1650-1700*, Wallingford, PA: Pendle Hill Publications, 1996

Tom Gates, *Members One of Another: The Dynamics of Membership in Quaker Meeting*, Wallingford, Pennsylvania: Pendle Hill Pamphlet 371, 2004

Thomas Hamm, *The Quakers in America*, New York: Columbia University Press, 2003

H. Larry Ingle, *Quakers in Conflict: The Hicksite Reformation*, Knoxville: The University of Tennessee Press, 1986

Suggested Reading List

Thomas R. Kelly, *A Testament of Devotion*, New York: Harper & Row, 1941

Patricia Loring, *Listening Spirituality, Volume 1: Personal Spiritual Practices Among Friends*, Washington: Openings Press, 1997 and *Listening Spirituality, Volume 2: Corporate Spiritual Practice Among Friends*, Washington: Openings Press, 1999

Donna McDaniel and Vanessa Julye, *Fit for Freedom, Not for Friendship: Quakers, African Americans, and the Myth of Racial Justice*, Philadelphia: Quaker Press of FGC, 2009

Rosemary Moore, *The Light in Their Consciences: The Early Quakers in Britain, 1646-1666*, University Park: The Pennsylvania State University Press, 2000

William Penn, *Primitive Christianity Revived*: Translated into Modern English by Paul Buckley, San Francisco: Inner Light Books, 2018

Isaac Penington, *Light Within and Selected Writings*, Philadelphia: The Tract Association of Friends, 1998

John Punshon, *Encounter with Silence: Reflections from the Quaker Tradition*, Richmond, Indiana: Friends United Press, 1987

William Taber, *Four Doors to Meeting for Worship*, Wallingford, Pennsylvania: Pendle Hill Pamphlet 306, 1992

Harold D. Weaver, Jr., Paul Kriese, and Stephen W. Angell (eds), *Black Fire: African American Quakers on Spirituality and Human Rights*. Philadelphia: Quaker Press of FGC, 2011

Lloyd Lee Wilson, *Quaker Vision of Gospel Order*, Burnsville, North Carolina: Celo Valley Books, 1993

Terry S. Wallace, *A Sincere and Constant Love: An Introduction to the Work of Margaret Fell*, 1992

John Woolman, *The Journal and Major Essays of John Woolman*, Edited by Phillips P. Moulton, New York: Oxford University Press, 1971

NOTES

[1] Postscript to an epistle addressed to "the brethren in the north" and issued by a meeting of elders at Balby in 1656, as printed in William C. Braithwaite, *Beginnings of Quakerism*, 1912, p. 311.

[2] Isaac Penington, "Some Misrepresentations of me concerning Church-Government." In *Works of the long-mournful and sorely-distressed Isaac Penington*, Volume 4, p. 378.

[3] John Woolman, "Some Considerations on the Keeping of Negroes." In John Woolman, *The Journal and Major Essays of John Woolman*, Phillips P. Moulton (ed), 1971, p. 236.

[4] George Fox, *Journal of George Fox*, J. I. Nickalls (ed), 1952, p. 263.

[5] William Penn, *Primitive Christianity Reviv'd*, Chapter 11, Section 7.

[6] All Bible quotes are from the New International Version except as noted.

[7] Isaac Penington, *Letters*, John Barclay (ed), 1828, p. 139.

[8] Parker J. Palmer, *A Place Called Community*, Pendle Hill Pamphlet 212, 1977, p. 20.

[9] Fran Taber in Frances and William Taber, *The Witness of Conservative Friends William and Frances Taber*, The Wider Quaker Fellowship, 2010, pp. 12-13.

[10] Margaret Fell, "Women's Speaking Justified," 1666. In Terry S. Wallace, *A Sincere and Constant Love: An Introduction to the Work of Margaret Fell*, 1992, p. 65.

[11] John Woolman, "Some Considerations on the Keeping of Negroes." In John Woolman, *The Journal and Major Essays of John Woolman*, Phillips P. Moulton (ed), 1971, p. 202.

[12] 1952 Proceedings of London Yearly Meeting.

[13] George Fox, *Collection of Many Select and Christian Epistles, Letters and Testimonies*. In *Works of George Fox (Volume 7 & 8)*, p. 91.

[14] Philip Gulley, *Living the Quaker Way*, Convergent Books, 2013, p. 132.

[15] George Fox, *Journal of George Fox*, J. I. Nickalls (ed), 1952, p. 65.

[16] *Declaration from the harmless & innocent people of God, called, Quakers*, 1660, p. 1.

Notes

[17] John Woolman, "A Plea for the Poor." In John Woolman, *The Journal and Major Essays of John Woolman*, Phillips P. Moulton (ed), 1971, p. 255.

[18] William Penn, *Some Fruits of Solitude*, 12.

[19] John Woolman, *The Journal and Major Essays of John Woolman*, Phillips P. Moulton (ed), 1971, p.28.

[20] Margaret Fell Fox, *Letter to Friends, Brethren, and Sisters*, April 1700. From manuscript Portfolio 25/66 in Library of the Religious Society of Friends, London.

[21] Thomas R. Kelly, *A Testament of Devotion*, New York: Harper & Row, 1941, p. 110.

[22] Faith and Practice of New England Yearly Meeting, 1985, p. 141.

[23] Edward Hicks, *Memoirs of the life and religious labors of Edward Hicks*, 1851, p. 363.

[24] John Woolman, "A Plea for the Poor." In John Woolman, *The Journal and Major Essays of John Woolman*, Phillips P. Moulton (ed), 1971, p. 265.

[25] Elizabeth Watson, "Parents and Children in the Quaker Home," *The Canadian Friend*, vol. 75, no. 5 (September-October 1979), pp. 14-15.

[26] Britain Yearly Meeting, *Quaker Book of Faith & Practice*, 1995-2020, Fifth Edition, 1.02.30.

[27] Elias Hicks, Dear Friend: Letters and Essays of Elias Hicks, San Francisco: Inner Light Books, 2011, p. 182.

[28] Faith and Practice of New England Yearly Meeting of Friends, 1985, p. 235.

[29] George Fox, *Journal of George Fox*, J. I. Nickalls (ed), 1952, p. 65.

[30] George Fox, *Journal of George Fox*, J. I. Nickalls (ed), 1952, p. 11.

[31] William C. Braithwaite, *The Beginnings of Quakerism*, Cambridge: University Press, 1961, pp. 50, 67

[32] William C. Braithwaite, *The Beginnings of Quakerism*, Cambridge: University Press, 1961, p. 152

INDEX

Abuse/Addiction
  Alcohol, 29, 34
  Domestic, 29
  Drugs, 29, 34
  Sexual, 29
Accumulation of Wealth, 33
Alcohol, 29, 34
American Friends Service Committee, 77
Associate Member. See Membership:Youth
Attenders, 52
Bereavement, 31
Bible, 3, 6, 11, 17, 49, 77
Braithwaite, William C., 82
Burial Grounds, 43, 69
Business Process, 37, 50, 55
  Query, 74
Capital Punishment, 21, 36
Care for Creation. See Testimonies, Seeking Harmony with Creation *and* Quaker Earthcare Witness
Cemetaries. *See* Burial Grounds
Children
  and Divorce, 30
  and Marriage, 62
  Birth of, 47
  Nurturing, 24, 27
  Offering Ministry, 5
  Religious Education, 7
  Setting an Example for, 24

Citizenship, 35
Civic Responsibilities, 35
Civil Disobedience, 35
Clearness Committees, 9, 27, 48, 66, 92
  for Marriage, 61, 62
  for Membership, 53, 55
Clerk
  Presiding, 44, 92, 97
  Duties, 37, 41, 65, 67, 74, 98
  Yearly Meeting, 70
  Recording, 38, 44, 64, 70
Close Relationships, 24
Community, Spiritual, 2, 3, 19, 24, 35, 39, 48, 50, 51, 54
  Query, 74
Corporate Discernment, 5
Death, 30
Death Penalty. *See* Capital Punishment
Divine Guidance, 1, 2, 3, 6, 7, 9, 11, 12, 13, 16, 17, 18, 19, 20, 21, 23, 24, 26, 27, 35, 37, 38, 46, 51, 77
  Query, 74
Divorce, 30
Ecclesiastical Endorsement, 66
Education
  Children, 25, 49, 93
  Religious, 49, 93
  Sex, 25
Elder, Eldering, 93

Index

Elders at Balby, 1
Employment. *See* Work in the World
Environment/Earthcare. *See* Testimonies, Seeking Harmony with Creation
Eternal Light. *See* Inward Light
Fell, Margaret, 16, 23, 82, 102
Fox, George, 13, 18, 19, 20, 77, 81, 93, 101
Friends Committee on National Legislation, 79
Friends General Conference, 55, 76
Friends Journal, 79
Friends World Committee for Consultation, 78
Friendships, 25
Gambling, 35
Gender Identity, 18, 25
God, 1, 6, 10, 12, 18, 19, 32, 37, 45, 46, 49, 51
 and Civil Disobedience, 35
 and Marriage, 26
 and Sexuality, 25
 in Business Meeting, 6
 in Everyone Query, 75
 in Worship, 3
 Love of, 22, 25
 Waiting on, 3
Gulley, Philip, 18
Handbook, 71, 94
Hicks, Edward, 24
Hicks, Elias, 31, 87

History
 Beginnings of Quakerism, 81
 in the American Colonies, 85
 Ohio Valley Yearly Meeting, 88
 Second Period, 86
Individual Spiritual Disciplines, 6
Inner Light. See Inward Light
Intervisitation, 67
 Letter of Introduction, 67
 Traveling Minute, 67, 71, 99
Inward Light, 1, 2, 18, 81, 83, 87, 94
 and Community, 2
 and Conflict, 21
 and Parenting, 28
 and Simplicity, 23
 Guidance of. *See* Divine Guidance
 in Business Meeting, 5, 38
 in Clearness, 9
 in the Home, 27
 in Worship, 3, 4
 Stand Still in, 19
Jesus, 2, 7, 11, 12, 20, 32
Jobs. *See* Work in the World
Kelly, Thomas R., 23, 102
Light of Christ. See Inward Light
Light Within. *See* Inward Light
Light, the. *See* Inward Light
Marriage, 26, 60, 96
 Ceremony, 63
 Certificate, 63
 Meeting for Worship for, 63
 of Non-members, 62
 Procedure, 60

Index

Meeting for Business
  Basis of, 1, 6, 37
  Purpose of, 37
  Query, 74
  Records of, 64
Meeting for Worship, 1, 3, 50, 95
  and Children, 29
  Fostering, 46, 92
  Gathered, 93
  Preparation for, 3
  Programmed, 97
  Query, 74
Membership, 51, 56, 57
  Application Process, 53, 54
  Children, 54
  Disownment from, 59
  Dual, 56
  Loss of Interest in, 58
  Preparation for, 52
  Resignation from, 58
  Sojourning, 56
  Termination of, 57
  Transfer of, 57
  Youth, 54
Minister, Recorded. *See* Recorded Minister
Ministry, Vocal. *See* Vocal Ministry
Minutes, 95
  Approval of, 38, 44, 46, 53, 94
  Preparation of, 38, 39, 42, 46, 53, 58
Minutes, Traveling. See Intervisitation

Monthly Meeting, 37, 43, 67, 90, 95
  Committees, 45
    Marriage Oversight, 61, 63, 96
    Ministry and Counsel, 46, 50, 53, 54, 55, 57, 58, 59, 61, 62, 65, 74, 92
    Outreach, 49
    Pastoral Care, 47, 96
  Establishment, 39
  Incorporation, 68
  Laying Down, 41
  Officers, 44
  Property, 41, 42, 44, 45, 65, 68
  Records, 64
  State of the Meeting Report, 50
  Treasurer, 34, 44
  Trusts, 69
Palmer, Parker J., 15
Penington, Isaac, 5, 15, 102
Penn, William, 22, 84, 85, 102, 110
Personal Finances. *See* Accumulation of Wealth
Prayer, 3, 4, 6, 27, 37, 38
Quaker Earthcare Witness, 80
Quaker United Nations Office, 79
Quaker Worship. *See* Meeting for Worship
QuakerSpeak, 80
Quarterly Meeting, 69, 97
  Establishment, 41
Queries, 73, 97

Index

Racism and Racial Prejudice, 17, 102
Recorded Minister, 66, 97
Recreation, 34
Released Friend, 97
Revision of Faith & Practice, 75
Scriptures. *See* Bible
Sexual Orientation, 18, 25
Sexuality, 25
Silent Worship. *See* Meeting for Worship
Sojourning Membership. See Membership, Sojourning
Spiritual Disciplines Query, 74
Spiritual Disciplines, Individual, 6
Spiritual Friendships, 10
Spiritual Practices, Other, 7
State of Society Report. *See* Yearly Meeting, State of Society Report
State of the Meeting Report. *See* Monthly Meeting, State of the Meeting Report
Statistical Reports, 73
Statistician, 98
  Monthly Meeting, 66
  Yearly Meeting, 70
Taber, Fran, 15
Testimonies, 13
  Community, 15
  Equality, 16
  Integrity, 18
  Peace, 19

Seeking Harmony with Creation, 22
Query, 75
Simplicity, 23
Stewardship, 31
Tobacco, 34
Treasurer, 34, 99
  Monthly Meeting, 44
  Yearly Meeting, 70, 72
Treatment of Civic Offenders, 36
Trustees, 34, 45, 69
Vocal Ministry, 1, 3, 4, 46, 50, 95, 96, 97, 99
Waiting Worship. *See* Meeeting for Worship
Watson, Elizabeth, 28
Woolman, John, 6, 17, 20, 22, 27, 86, 88, 102
Work in the World, 32
Worship Group, 39, 100
Worship Sharing, 7
Yearly Meeting, 70, 100
  Committees, 70
    Budget and Finance, 68
    Executive, 67, 68, 71, 73, 95
    Nominating, 73
    Religious Nurture and Education, 51
  Composition of, 70
  Minute Book, 51
  Officers, 70
  Records, 64
  Representatives to, 70
  State of Society Report, 51
Youth Member. See Membership:Youth

www.ingramcontent.com/pod-product-compliance
Lightning Source LLC
Chambersburg PA
CBHW072205100526
44589CB00015B/2369